Tom

from

Mom and Dad

September 12, 1986

To my father, Abraham Leifer

NEIL LEIFER'S SPORTS STARS

Text by Peter Bonventre, ABC Sports

Foreword by Roone Arledge, President of ABC Sports & News

Designed by J.C. Suarès

A DOLPHIN BOOK
DOUBLEDAY & COMPANY, INC.
GARDEN CITY, NEW YORK
1985

FRONT ENDPAPERS
*Gymnasts Koji Gushiken of Japan and Peter
Vidmar of the USA.*

TITLE PAGE
*Muhammad Ali and Joe Frazier flank promoter
Don King.*

BACK ENDPAPERS
*Willie Mays, No. 24, signs autographs for
New York Mets' fans.*

A Dolphin Book
Photographs Copyright © 1985 by Neil Leifer
Text Copyright © 1985 by Peter Bonventre
All Rights Reserved
Printed in the United States of America
First Edition

The following publishers have generously given permission
to use extended quotations from copyrighted works:
Page 52, from "There Must Be Something Inside." © copy-
right 1984 PKM Music. Pages 126, 130, from *The New
Yorker.* Reprinted by permission; © Herbert Warren Wind.
Originally in *The New Yorker.* Page 217, from the *New
York Times.* Copyright © 1970 by The New York Times
Company. Reprinted by permission.

Library of Congress Cataloging in Publication Data

Leifer, Neil.
    Neil Leifer's Sports stars.

    "A Dolphin book."
    Includes index.
    1. Athletes—Biography.   2. Athletes—Pictorial works.
I. Bonventre, Peter.   II. Title.   III. Title: Sports
stars.
GV697.A1L417   1985   796'.092'2 [B]   85-6737
ISBN 0-385-19562-1

Photographic prints from this book
are available through:
Photographics Unlimited
69 Fairview Drive
Albertson, NY 11507

Photographs from this book
are available for reuse through:
Sports Illustrated Pictures
Time & Life Building, 19th floor
Rockefeller Center
New York, NY 10020
Tel.: (212) 841-3663

CONTENTS

Foreword
6

Introduction
10

Jim Brown
44

Chris Evert-Lloyd
48

Sam Huff
50

Pete Rose
52

Nadia Comaneci
54

Muhammad Ali
56

Angel Cordero
68

Vasili Alexeyev
70

Sonny Liston
74

John McEnroe
76

Mark Spitz
80

Bear Bryant
84

Hank Aaron
90

Eric Heiden
92

O.J. Simpson
94

Joe DiMaggio
102

Dorothy Hamill
104

Mario Andretti
106

Mary Lou Retton
108

Roger Maris
112

Roger Staubach
116

Secretariat
118

Mickey Mantle
122

Jack Nicklaus
126

Pelé
132

Oakland A's
134

Nate Archibald
136

Wayne Gretzky
138

Tom Watson
140

Roberto Clemente
142

Bill Shoemaker
144

Kareem Abdul-Jabbar
146

Bjorn Borg
150

Sugar Ray Robinson
156

Sandy Koufax
158

Jimmy Connors
162

Arnold Palmer
164

Reggie Jackson
166

Joe Namath
168

Casey Stengel
174

Bill Johnson
180

Steve Cauthen
182

Tom Seaver
186

Wilt Chamberlain
190

Sugar Ray Leonard
192

Willie Mays
196

Starr, Hornung, Taylor
200

Julius Erving
206

Martina Navratilova
208

Joe Frazier
212

Vince Lombardi
214

Gerry Cooney
218

Daley Thompson
220

Terry Bradshaw
224

Carl Lewis
226

Bill Bradley
232

Billy Kidd
236

Ray Nitschke
240

Gordie Howe
244

Debbie Armstrong
246

Y.A. Tittle
248

Valerie Brisco-Hooks
250

FOREWORD

by Roone Arledge

My introduction to Neil came in 1961. I was in Moscow producing the USA versus USSR track meet for ABC Sports' brand-new program, "Wide World of Sports." During my survey of Lenin Stadium I noticed a photographer wandering around the Stadium with three cameras hanging from his neck. I really didn't pay much attention to him. I had my hands full dealing with the Russians and the complexity of our coverage. This was the first time that American television cameras were allowed into the Soviet Union for an event of this kind, and we had flown tons of equipment into Moscow since the Russian and American television systems were not compatible.

The Russians warned all journalists and cameramen to stay off certain areas of the field during the competition. Neil, courageous even at the age of 18, ignored the warning. Valeri Brumel, the great Russian high jumper, was preparing for his jump and Neil was standing next to him. The Russians were astonished.

So were we. Mike Freedman, a great ABC cameraman who was pioneering a new device called the "handheld camera," was soon standing next to Neil, delivering fantastic closeups.

At the end of the day the American and Russian athletes jogged in pairs around the track with their hands locked in sportsmanship. Neil was in front of them, jogging backwards; Mike was lying on the track, with the athletes jogging over him. Mike and Neil spent that day, and the next 25 years, fighting for the perfect position at the great sports events around the world.

Neil's innovative approach to sports photography has inspired our cameramen at many events since that warm day in Moscow. We have joined him under water and in the air. At times Neil or one of his counterparts led the way, and at other times we led. In all cases we all benefited. The contribution made to television by the great still photographers cannot be overstated. For this reason, Neil's success cannot be measured entirely by this collection of photographs.

It is ironic that Neil did not notice the advancement of sports television until a Monday Night Football game when it literally tapped him on the shoulder. As he was focusing on

Bob Brown, the mammoth offensive lineman for the Oakland Raiders, he was bumped from behind by an ABC cameraman toting a handheld camera. Millions of Americans were seeing the shot live on national television. He realized at that moment that he would never be alone again.

There was a small group of journalists covering sports events back in the 1960s. We learned from each other. You were sure to see the same people week after week. It seems that Neil was always in our shot. There is a simple reason for that: he was always in the right place. It was during those days I grew to appreciate Neil's work.

As I page through this book I am swept by memories. Over the years I have had the pleasure of working with many of the athletes, and I have worked at many of the events featured on these pages. In some instances I, like you, have simply had the pleasure of viewing the photographs in a magazine or watching the event on television. In all cases, I am indebted to Neil for preserving these memories.

This book is more than a pictorial history of sports. It is a documentation of the great moments, the great personalities and the great memories of the past 25 years.

Captured forever in this collection are the classic stance of Mickey Mantle, the perfect drop back pass of Joe Namath, the pose of Eric Heiden at the starting line and the solitude of the mammoth Alexeyev over the barbell. Each is a subject of calm and controlled energy. Each is an explosion waiting to be ignited.

These photographs evoke memories beyond the obvious; I recall sights, sounds and emotions. Memories that are personal to each of us: Mantle rounding the basepads, slapping hands with fellow players and coaches in pinstripes; Namath thrusting his finger into the air after acting out the miracle he had so boldly predicted in Super Bowl III; Heiden's powerful legs pushing him to the gold medal in five events at the Olympic Oval in Lake Placid; Alexeyev's distinct groan accompanying a world-record lift.

It is not surprising that Neil's best-known photographs document historic moments in sport. Perhaps his most widely acclaimed photo is Muhammad Ali hovering over the fallen champion, Sonny Liston, in 1965. It is the perfect picture catching the emotion of a distraught Ali urging the champion to get up and fight. The photo has become a part of history. In the minds of many boxing fans, it *is* the fight.

Other pictures throughout this book have become synonymous with the events themselves. The photo of O.J. Simpson accepting the game ball from an official will always represent O.J.'s 2,000-yard season. When I think of Bjorn Borg's first Wimbledon title, I will remember him on his knees, finally allowing his emotions to flow. The infamous *"no mas"* fight will forever provoke memories of Sugar Ray Leonard's celebration and Roberto Duran's lonely retreat to his corner. Vince Lombardi's ride atop Jerry Kramer's shoulder is a huge part of my memory of the second Super Bowl.

There is another type of photograph found throughout Neil's collection. It is the posed shot. These pictures are special because they equally reflect the personality of the subject and the talent of the photographer. Examine, for a moment, Casey Stengel's face. You will find a quarter of a century of baseball history: I see seven Yankee world championship teams and Don Larsen's perfect game in the 1956 World Series. I see Stengel on the bench, legs crossed—a picture of serenity. I see a man thankful that he can spend his days managing baseball for a living. And finally, I hear his doubletalk, "Stengelese," and I remember his wink.

I see much of the same in Bear Bryant's face, hidden under his hound's tooth hat, the lines of his face as evident and as significant as the yard markers lining his classroom. He is perfectly posed with chalk in his hand, explaining the game to his pupils. As I look at this picture, I strain to hear his mumbling. For a man who never spoke clearly, he was never misunderstood.

Muhammad Ali spoke clearly, eloquently and often. He was that rare athlete who was as comfortable outside the perimeter of his sport as inside. He wore a tuxedo as comfortably as he wore his shorts and tassled boots. The picture that opens this book is vintage Ali. The smile, as much a trademark as his lightning-quick jab, is evident. I hear his sweet voice rhyming "float like a butterfly. . . ." Not everyone agreed with Ali, but we were all seduced by him.

Neil and I have shared the experience of countless events since we first met in 1961.

I have always been impressed with his determination to get the perfect shot.

During the year before the 1984 Olympic Games, he shot 14 Olympic athletes, each in his or her home country. It is no small task to get a Chinese gymnast to pose on the Great Wall of China in the dead of winter. Nor is it easy to assemble the Indian field hockey team in front of the Taj Mahal. One can only imagine the difficulty involved in posing Koji Gushikin on the rings in front of majestic Mount Fuji. The photograph of the twins running past the giraffes in Kenya was recorded only with the help of a game warden, a bundle of food and 30 rolls of film.

The Olympic project took a full year and severely tested Neil's ingenuity and determination. Neil wanted to photograph Daley Thompson running past Windsor Castle. But Daley pulled his groin the day before the shoot and was unable to run. Neil improvised and placed Daley with a guard at the Palace. The Thompson wit was intact. If you look closely you will see the guard violating the strict code of the Palace Gate; he is laughing. This is easy to understand since Daley made us all laugh during the Olympic summer in Los Angeles.

Neil's determination paid off in his bid to photograph Fidel Castro. After months of lobbying with Cuban officials, he was, to his surprise, granted a session. Neil requested only that the great heavyweight Teofilo Stevenson be present to pose with the President. He was surprised to find half of the Cuban Olympic team in the stadium to pose as well.

But determination alone does not make a photographer great. Neil combines a number of qualities. These qualities are best illustrated in the photograph of the George Forman–Ali fight in Zaire. Luck. Foreman landed perfectly on the canvas. Ingenuity. The view offered by the overhead camera. Skill. The picture was perfectly framed and timed.

Although Neil has never paid an athlete to pose, he does admit to a few compromises over the years. In order to get Castro to pose, Neil had to promise the Cuban leader that he would be the only nonathlete in the Olympic essay as well as in this book. Well, it didn't turn out exactly that way. On the last page is a picture from Neil's private collection; Castro is lighting Neil's cigar.

This cameo, I think, is well deserved.

INTRODUCTION

AMERICA JUMPS FOR JOY

In his office high atop Park Avenue in New York, the new commissioner of baseball sat with his feet on his desk. Blue-eyed and sandy-haired, he wore a button-down shirt and an ordinary maroon tie that highlighted his boyish face and easy smile. At 47, he gave the impression of a man who had spent his working days on a college campus, guiding eager students, or perhaps in a small-town hospital, tending to his patients in a firm but reassuring bedside manner.

Then the questioning began, and Peter Ueberroth spoke softly and deliberately in a flat voice. He came at answers slowly, hedging, digressing, stalling artfully until he figured out what he wanted to say. He threw sliders, not fastballs, and at times it was hard to imagine that this was the same brash entrepreneur who had made millions in the travel business—and masterminded the extraordinary spectacle that was the 1984 Olympic Games in Los Angeles.

According to *Time* magazine, which named him Man of the Year for his Olympian achievement, Ueberroth once described himself as both shy and ruthless. Even old friends have called him a fascinating paradox, and to reporters covering the Olympics he alternately appeared as a hopeless idealist, a cunning businessman, a noble sportsman, and a petty tyrant. Somehow, though, the contradictions within Ueberroth mixed well enough to make him exactly right for the job of president of the Los Angeles Olympic Organizing Committee.

From the beginning, Ueberroth knew he couldn't count on the city of Los Angeles, which had passed a resolution denying municipal funds to its own Olympic Games. Thus, when he started, Ueberroth not only had no staff, he had no money. No sweat. It was 1978, and he had six years to prepare for a two-week extravaganza. A lifetime. First, he'd hire the best people he could find. Then, he'd stretch his managerial gifts to the limits, leading and inspiring and turning his mission into a shimmering crusade.

Ueberroth promptly dismissed the cynics who predicted that the Olympics were too expensive and too political to survive. He believed the Olympics could be saved and that he could save them. He'd show the doomsayers what this country was made of. He'd raise the necessary money through television rights, corporate sponsorship and ticket sales. In addition to his hired hands, he'd eventually recruit 72,000 volunteers and energize them with his unflagging spirit and self-confidence. He'd put his faith in the support of the American people—and he'd pray for a lot of luck.

For the first time in a generation, the
LA Olympics brought pride, optimism—and a $215-million surplus.

Egypt's Muhammad Neguib in the shadow of the Sphinx.

PAGES 18–19.
Jin-Ho Kim in front of an ancient Korean palace.

PAGES 20–21.
Japan's Koji Gushiken framed against Mount Fuji.

PAGES 22–23.
Sophia Sakorafa of Greece at the Parthenon.

Kristin Otto on the steps of East Germany's monument to its unknown soldier.

PAGES 26–27.
India's famed field hockey team in front of the Taj Mahal.

Sebastian Coe of Great Britain on the road to Windsor Castle.

PAGES 30–31. Kipkoech Cheruiyot and his twin brother Charlie on the plains of Kenya.

PAGES 32–33. Superheavyweight boxer Francesco Damiani at the Colosseum in Rome.

Mary Decker at Mount Rushmore in South Dakota.

PAGES 36–37.
Gymnast Qiurui Zhou at the Great Wall of China.

PAGES 38–39.
Cuba's superheavy-weight champion Teofilo Stevenson and El Commandante Fidel Castro.

Let's pause and remember when Chris Evert-Lloyd was sweet 16, and everybody called her Chrissie. She wore brightly colored ribbons in her hair, and every time she pursed her lips in determination and waved her two-fisted backhand with nothing to lose, she sent ripples of excitement through the staid old West Side Tennis Club in Forest Hills. For one giddy, glorious week, she held the 1971 U.S. Open in the palm of her hand—and it seemed that all who saw her began to believe in fairy tales coming true.

Playing with poise and grace beyond her years, Chrissie easily beat Edda Buding, then overcame almost certain disaster to upset Mary Ann Eisel Curtis, 4–6, 7–6, 6–1, coolly staving off six match points in the second set with long forehands and backhands that landed just in. Then, she came from behind twice more to defeat Francoise Durr (2–6, 6–2, 6–3) and Leslie Hunt (4–6, 6–2, 6–3) in a pair of groundstroke duels that drove the crowds wild. In both matches, she stayed at the baseline and kept hitting two-handed backhands and crisp forehands that ran her opponents from side to side until they wilted. When they came in, she hit past them. When they stayed back, she marooned them with drop shots that fell dead on the grass.

Chrissie's magical streak ended in the semifinals, where she met top-seeded Billie Jean King, 27 years old and a Wimbledon champion. In the first set, each held service until Mrs. King, trailing 2–3, broke through and won seven straight games. Billie Jean's powerful serve-and-volley attack exposed Chrissie's weaknesses on grass, and her spinning ground strokes and deft lobs disrupted the rhythm of the teenager's smooth, patterned game. She won in straight sets (6–3, 6–2), and as they walked off the court together, Billie Jean put her arm around Chrissie and said, "Don't let it bother you, Chrissie. You've got a whole life ahead of you."

"I've got a lot to learn and develop," Chrissie said later, "but I can be No. 1. If I don't make it at, say, 19, I'll try to make it at 20. And just keep going."

Chris had to be No. 1: "If I don't make it at, say, 19, I'll try to make it at 20. And just keep going."

SAM HUFF

On November 30, 1959, Sam Huff appeared on the cover of *Time* magazine. He had just turned 25, a 230-pound middle linebacker with the New York Giants who epitomized the violent world of pro football—and the raw strength and subtle scheming that was turning faceless defensive behemoths into genuine sports heroes. As the editors of *Time* breathlessly proclaimed: "Sunday after Sunday, pro quarterbacks have learned that whatever play they call, Sam Huff is likely to be in front of it. Huff is strong enough to flatten a plunging fullback such as the Chicago Bears' Rick Casares (6 feet 2½ inches, 225 pounds), swift enough to recover from a block in time to nail a halfback sprinting around end, smart enough to diagnose pass patterns and throw an offensive end off stride with an artful shoulder. But Huff is at his rugged best when he knifes through the line and 'red-dogs' a quarterback as he fades to pass. The crash of Huff's tackle can stir the Giant bench to bellowing glee and set the rabid fans in Yankee Stadium to rumbling out their own rapid-fire cheer like the chugging of a steam engine, 'Huff-Huff-Huff-Huff-Huff.' When Sam is on the field, the toughest fans of the U.S.'s toughest sport see what they came to see."

In the revered New York Giant defense, Huff became the epitome of the era's fearsome middle linebackers.

PETE ROSE

Going into the 1985 season, Pete Rose spoke confidently about breaking Ty Cobb's major-league record of 4,191 hits. As player-manager of the Cincinnati Reds, he expected to play himself every day, barring a disastrous slump, and estimated he would get the 95 hits he needed to surpass Cobb by August. Others weren't so sure. Rose was 44, they noted, and in baseball's modern era only one player of the same age had collected as many hits in a single season. That player was Sammy Rice, an outfielder who had stroked 98 hits for the Cleveland Indians in 1934.

Such trivia couldn't change Terry Cashman's mind. A singer-songwriter with a passion for sports, especially baseball, Cashman had popularized numerous tunes, including "One Stop Along the Way" about Johnny Bench, and "Willie, Mickey, and the Duke" in celebration of Mays, Mantle, and Snider. So convinced was Cashman of Rose's ultimate conquest of Cobb that he composed a tribute to the future Hall of Famer. "Pete heard the song and loved it," he said. "I intend to time its release with the pinnacle of Pete's drive for the record, when he's got 10 or 15 hits to go. That way, I hope, it will build and become synonymous with the event."

It's a different kind of song for me. I usually write ballads about baseball that reflect the summery and whimsical feelings I have for the game. But Pete is a blue-collar, never-say-die kind of guy, and I wanted a hard-driving beat to capture the essence of the man."

Cashman called his song "There Must Be Something Inside"—and provided these lyrics in advance of its release:

There must be something inside
Must be a heart beating wild
Filled with a burning desire
Must be a dream in his head
One day a voice must have said
Fatigue is a liar.

As player-manager of the Reds, Rose expected
to play himself every day—and pass Cobb's
mark of 4,191 hits.

NADIA COMANECI

Nadia!

To this day, the mere mention of her name still reminds us of magical moments and soaring flights of perfection. Nadia Comaneci was only 14 when she took our hearts away, a doll-like heroine from Russia who turned the XXI Olympiad into a theater of joy.

Every time Nadia approached an exercise, a hush came over the capacity crowds. It was always the same. Seconds into her routine, she was off on a journey that left all around her gasping, then cheering in a crescendo as she reached new heights of gymnastic genius. Nobody had ever witnessed a perfect 10-point score in Olympic competition, and here was Nadia rolling up one after another. Strength and flexibility, intelligence and courage, these were Nadia's virtues, but they didn't begin to explain her artistry. At times, she was motionless, freezing her 86-pound body above bars and beams. When others hesitated, she grew even bolder, picking up the tempo—flipping, twisting, leaping in a breathtaking blur of arms and legs. A ballerina in midair.

Nadia ended up with seven perfect 10-point scores and three gold medals, and sometimes it was easy to forget that she was very much like a lot of other kids who collect dolls and struggle with homework. She was polite and curious, and she was shy around reporters, answering questions in halting, childlike phrases that prompted *Newsweek*'s Pete Axthelm to write: "There is probably no speech in any language to describe the feeling of being 14—and perfect at what you do."

Why ask for words when so little was left to say? The eloquence of Nadia's performance spoke for itself—and would continue to speak to each new generation of athletes and tell them all they need to know about the 1976 Olympic Games in Montreal.

It was easy to forget that Nadia was like other kids who collect dolls and struggle with homework.

MUHAMMAD ALI

Muhammad Ali *was* the greatest.

In the beginning, he was Cassius Clay, and he mesmerized us with his grace and guile. He whipped big, bad Sonny Liston for the heavyweight title in 1964, then changed his religion and his name. In 1967, he refused to serve in an army that was fighting a war he opposed, and he paid the price: a 3½-year exile that cost him his prime as a fighter. When he returned, still marvelous but mortal, he took the blows with courage and style. He became champ again by outsmarting George Foreman in 1974, waged three bloody battles with Joe Frazier, then lost the crown to Leon Spinks and regained it seven months later.

Throughout the often joyous journey, no athlete ever dominated our attention quite the way Ali did. He seemed the embodiment of the tumultuous '60s, a symbol of pro-black, antiwar attitudes, a prism through which a generation viewed its world. He constantly amused or outraged us by switching roles—clown and martyr, preacher and poet, philosopher and savior—and he gradually fused all those roles into a single persona that was as complex as it was cosmic. He was always larger than the ring in which he floated. He knew that, and he loved it. That was why he continued to fight, leaving pieces of himself in Miami and Zaire, in New York and Manila. He absorbed the punishment to stay in the spotlight—and again he's paying the price.

In September, 1984, a 42-year-old Ali checked himself into a New York hospital. His illness was diagnosed as Parkinson's syndrome, a collection of symptoms similar, but not identical, to the disease of that name. The signs had long

On November 22, 1965, Ali taunted and humiliated ex-champ Floyd Patterson before knocking him out.

PAGE 56.
On February 25, 1964, Ali stung Liston into submission to capture the heavyweight title in Miami.

PAGE 57.
On October 1, 1975, Ali beat Frazier in an epic contest of wills that was called the "Thrilla in Manila."

PAGES 58–59.
On May 25, 1965, in a place called Lewiston in Maine, Ali retained his title by decking Liston in round one.

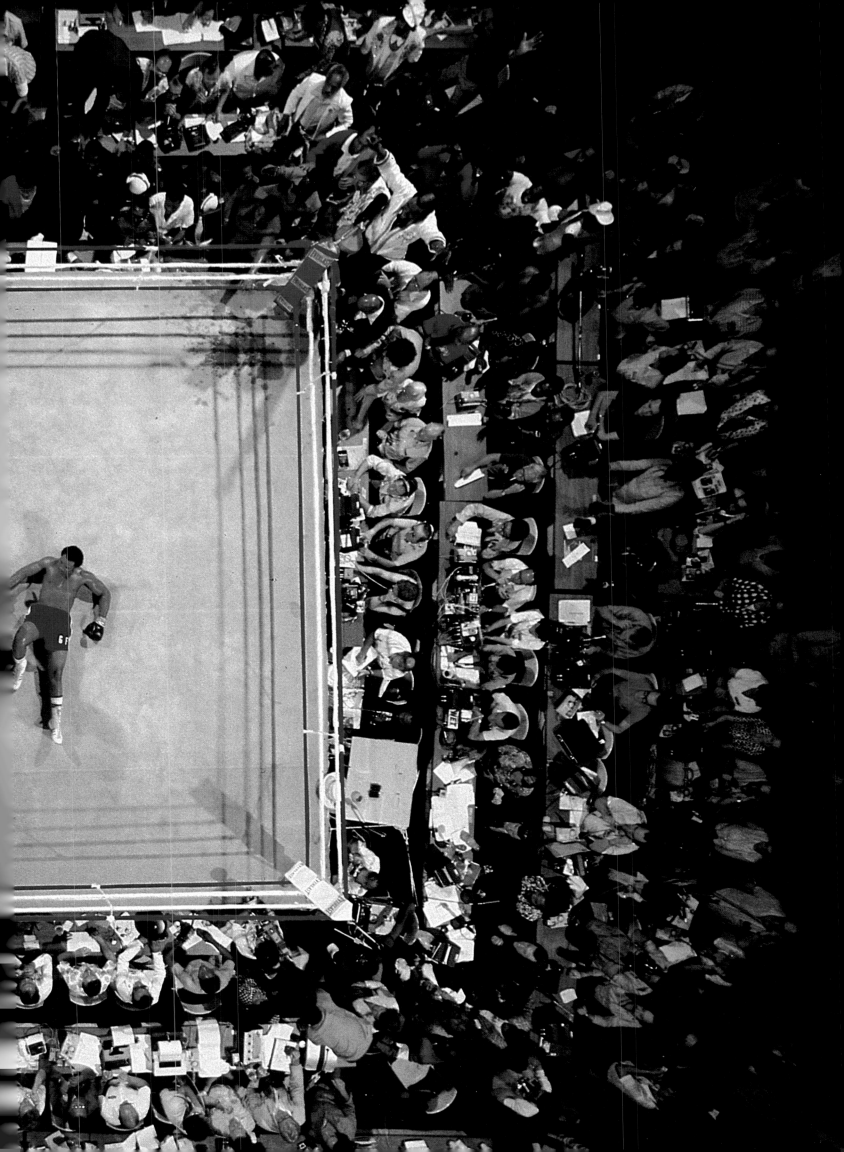

*Ali: "I'm so pretty. And I'm gonna stay pretty
'cause there ain't a fighter on earth fast
enough to hit me."*

"It's time for me to face another test. Things have been going too good lately. Allah must make me pay for all this fame and power. Somebody may shoot at me, who knows? I might be kidnapped and told to renounce the Muslims publicly or else be shot. And I'll have to say, 'Okay, shoot me.' Allah's always testing you. He don't let you get great for nothing. It ain't no accident that I'm the greatest man in the world at this time in history. I'm on a divine mission."

"When you can whip any man in the world, you never know peace."

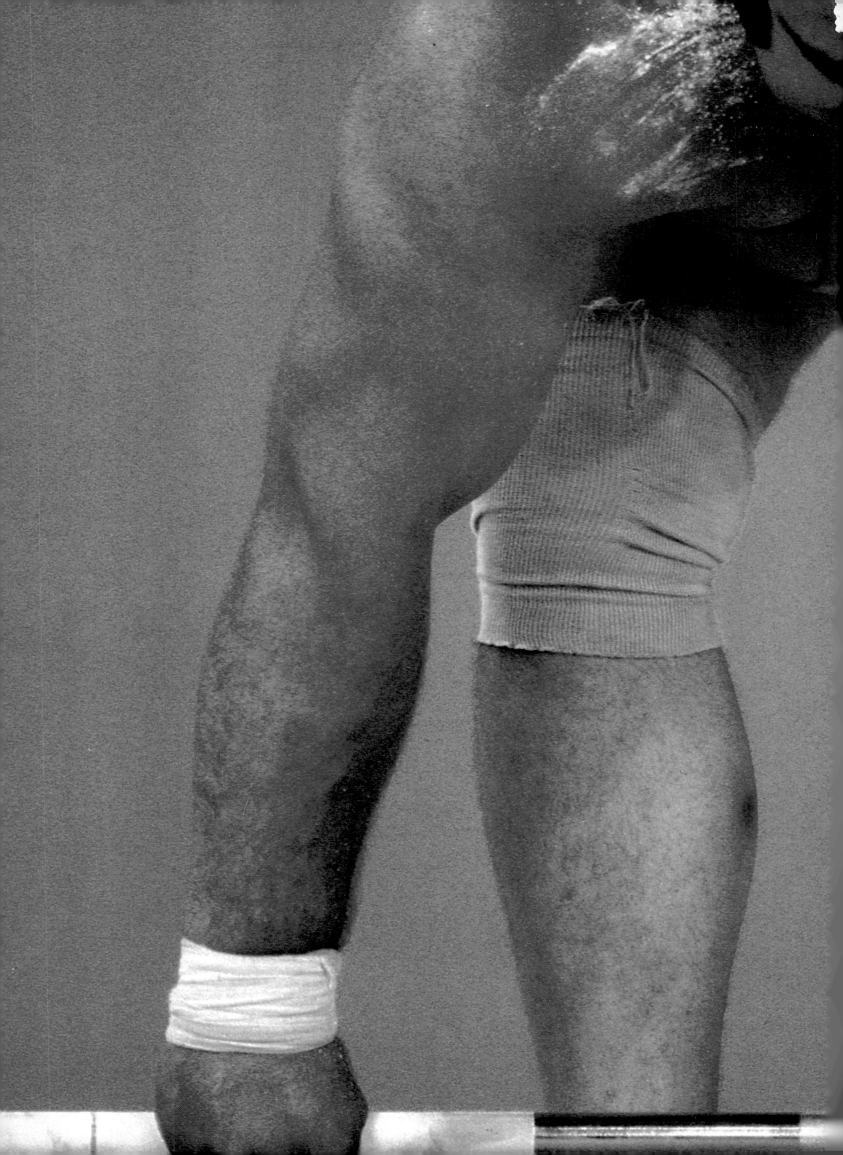

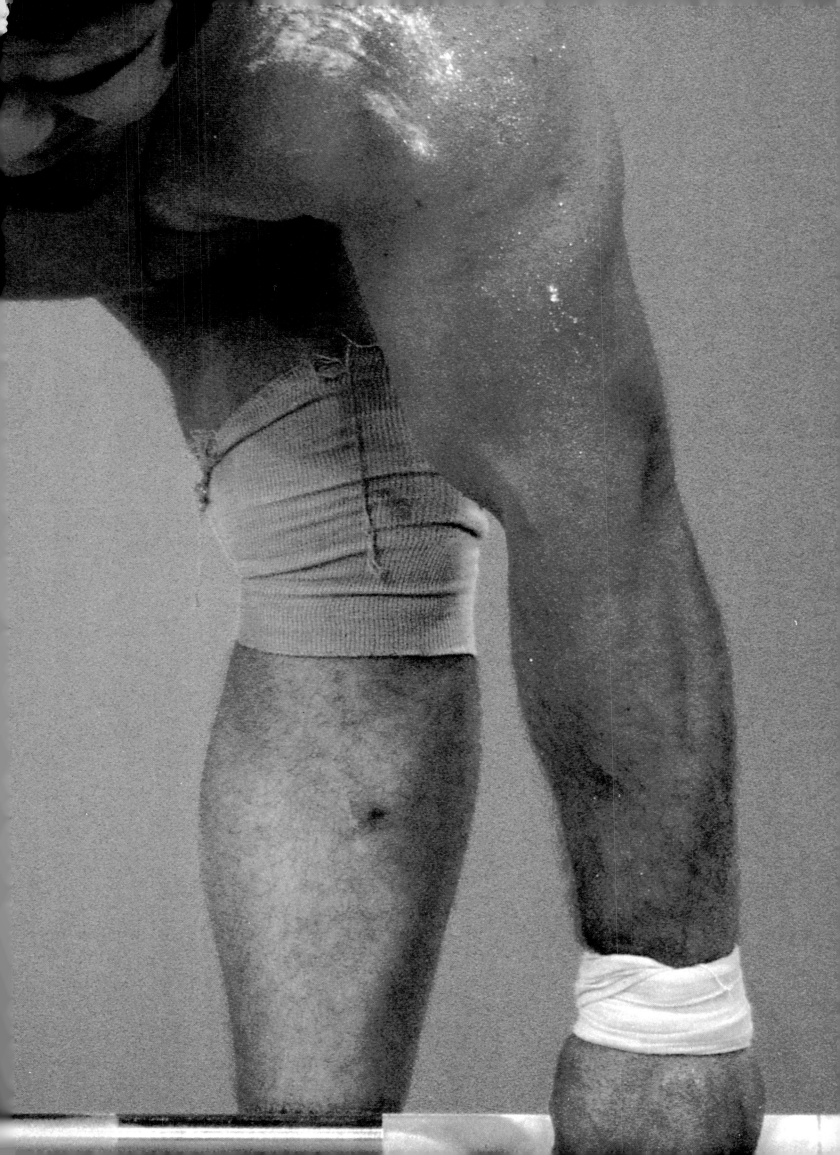

SONNY LISTON

He was raised in poverty, whipped almost daily by his father, unable to read or write, arrested 19 times, and convicted twice, serving time in the state penitentiary at Jefferson City, Missouri, where he learned to box. At 30, he knocked out Floyd Patterson to win the heavyweight championship, then lost the title to young Cassius Clay in Miami Beach on February 25, 1964.

Seven years later, Charles (Sonny) Liston was found dead in his Las Vegas home. Official cause of death: an overdose of heroin.

Harold Conrad doesn't believe Liston OD'd. Murder, he says. The publicist for four of Liston's fights, Conrad has often discussed and written about the fighter's death. "Sonny was scared to death of needles. I remember when he was training for the second Ali fight and was coming down with the flu. The doc was going to give him a shot of B_{12}, but when Sonny got a flash of that needle, he wanted to throw the doc out the window. Another thing, Sonny was a heavy boozer, and heroin isn't a boozer's bag. He smoked a little pot and did a little snorting, but he never went for hard drugs.

"When Sonny retired from the ring he had some dough stashed, but not very much, and he was looking for action. Some very tough citizens were running a loan-shark factory out of East Las Vegas, and since Sonny used to be a head knocker for the unions around St. Louis, they figured he'd make a perfect collector, and they hired him. But he wasn't satisfied. He wanted a bigger piece of the action. Meanwhile, Sonny was getting drunk around town, making scenes and putting pressure on these guys. Being the former heavyweight champion of the world doesn't cut any ice with the Shylocks. They're not about to let anybody cut into their turf. So one night they took him out to a party. After he got stinking drunk, they took him home, jabbed him with an OD, and that's the end of Sonny.

"I talked to a guy I knew in the Vegas sheriff's office, and here's what he said: 'A bad nigger. He got what was coming to him.' I don't buy that. He had some good qualities, but I think he died the day he was born."

Harold Conrad on Sonny Liston: "He had some good qualities, but I think he died the day he was born."

BEAR BRYANT

In later years, when asked why he wouldn't quit coaching, Bryant said, "Quit? I'd croak in a week."

Paul (Bear) Bryant liked his whiskey neat and his players lean. As the years rolled by, his pleated face and houndstooth hat became as much a part of the American landscape as the game he loved and worked at so hard. He got his nickname in high school when he accepted a dare to wrestle a bear, and it stuck for life. Recruited by Alabama, he played right end. After serving in the Navy during World War II, he took the job of head coach at Maryland, then moved on to Kentucky and Texas A & M before returning to his alma mater in 1958. Once a staunch segregationist, he waited until 1970 to sign his first black player—and later apologized for waiting so long. It was simply a matter of upbringing, he said, admitting that he didn't know any better.

At Alabama, Bryant's stern leadership produced six national titles and a record 24 straight postseason appearances in bowl games. When his time came to quit the sidelines, he had more victories (323–85–17) than any coach in the history of college football. In Bryant's opinion, too little credit was given to players like Joe Namath and Kenny Stabler and Lee Roy Jordan. As for the people of Alabama, they said an atheist was someone who didn't believe in Bear Bryant.

One who knew Bryant well was John Underwood, the co-author of the coach's autobiography, *Bear.* "The first time I met him," Underwood said, "he was leaning against a fence at practice the day before a big game against Georgia. I had heard so many horror stories about him, how tough he was and forbidding. I introduced myself. We started chatting, and I found him to be engaging and quite candid. He invited me to talk some more with him that night at his hotel room. When I got there, he was wearing red-striped pajamas, and I asked him if it was too late. He said, 'No, I sleep like a baby before a game—but I haven't taken my sleeping pill yet.'

"We talked for about four hours and really hit it off. After that, whenever I'd let him know I was coming to a game, he'd usually ask me to have dinner with him. When I got to know him even better, I told him I wanted to write an inside story for my magazine, *Sports Illustrated,* spend an entire week with him and attend practices and team meetings. To get that close to Bear was unheard of then, but he agreed. What I came away with was a lasting impression of his incredible ability to communicate. On the morning of the game, I was standing next to a professor at a team meeting. Bear always invited a couple of professors on these occasions. He spoke very softly when he was serious. The players had to lean forward to hear him. I couldn't believe how enraptured they were by him. One player accidentally knocked over a glass of water on the carpeted floor, and it sounded like Niag-

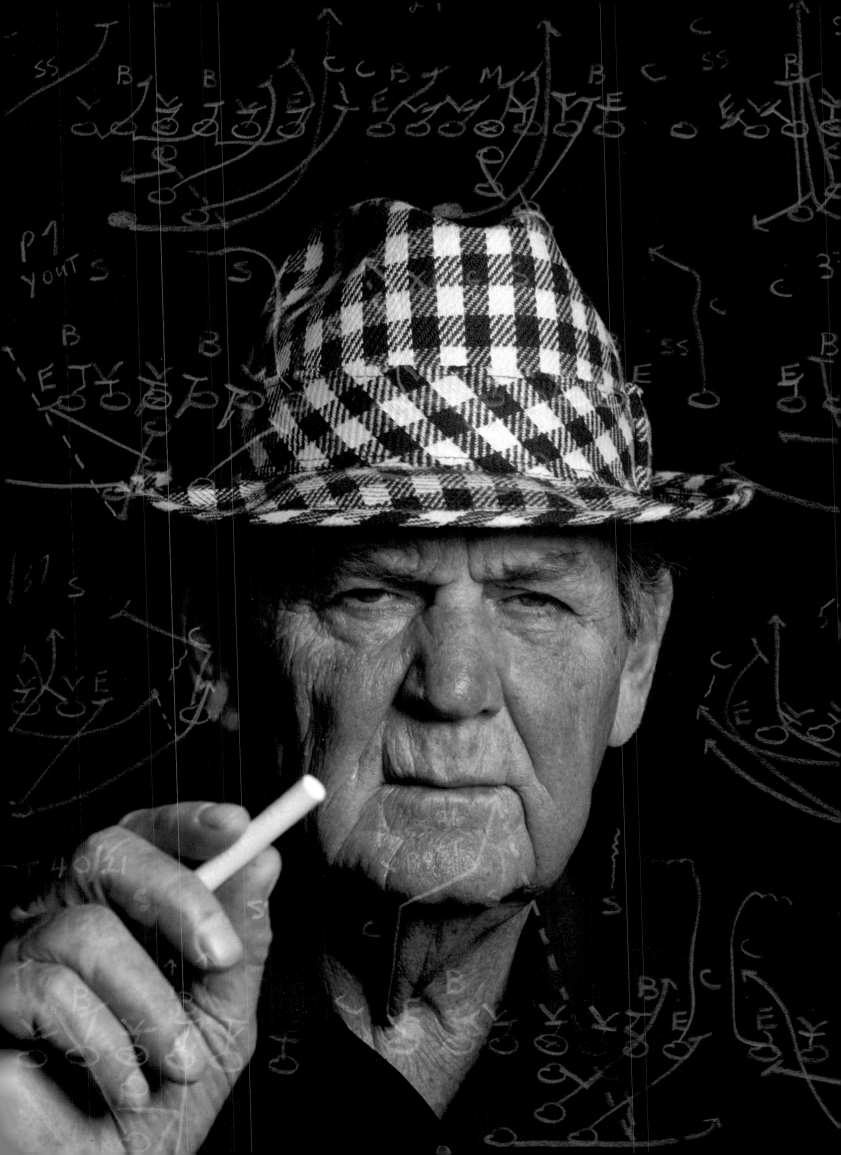

ahead – 1– 4 –5 – 4–12 –19 –22 –25
Behind – 2 – 5 – 10? –16 –17 –18 –21 –25 –26 –28

E. Bradrow – mallard – Clark – Jones – white
T. Cagana – ma dell – Seary – Cowell
D. allison – Robbins – Vissan deleave
C. matt – Robbins – Doreen Haleak – Jackson
M. Connell – Callier – Bramlett

T. Beasley – Searcy – Brown Cogale
E. Jacob – Gray – Caley – Sewin – Landrum
Q. Kraut – Callier – Brown – Gregson askewie
L. Jones – Simon – Patrick arentz Irerson
F. Jackson – Ferguson – Hill – William – wilder
R. aguivia – Nix – carter wilder

E. denies mann petter wood Burress
S. Scott Jones Russell
T. Bragg Haman Shim
M. Tyler cline llion edwards
T. cline Haman Castille
W. Boyd Laure Hill wood
E. Simon Pette mann wood

L.H. Castille – Tucker – Henderson Caley
R.H. Clements – Tucker – sprinsle Caley
S S Walcott – Harris – Jewin Gay.
S Tucker – Harris – sprinkle – Jervin

·Dont Forget·

Use time outs Intelligently –
Double time outs
R… clock Screen last play

Shift to punt -
Shift from punt - Run play
Expect Fla. onside kick
All Balance with formations -
Shift - motion
1 Play Pass -

Quick Screen - Crosses -
1 Play for Pass - Mallard -
two wide Ends -
Miss directions - trap - option
Tech Shotgun - mike take
remaining back - delay or draw -
Forward lateral - Lateral -
Expect unexpected -
at all times -
unbalanced - cleat - automatic -
Count changes personal when
we punt -
" 4d middle field for 7.D.
Kick Soft astro turn -

ara Falls. I realized then that Bear didn't coach football, he coached people. After the meeting, one professor said to me, 'I'd teach for nothing if I could hold my students like that.'

"Bear returned his players' respect in kind. He was the most loyal and caring coach I ever met. The quarterback on his first national championship team at Alabama was Pat Trammell. Trammell died of cancer. When he was going to Memorial Sloan-Kettering Hospital in New York for the first time, he asked Bear to go with him. Bear went, and Trammell had the operation. He went back to Alabama for law school. One afternoon, Bear saw Trammell standing at the edge of the practice field, and he looked terrible. 'I've got it again,' he told Bear. He went into an Alabama hospital. Not long after that, Bear had to make a television appearance in Birmingham, but he kept finding himself wanting to turn around and go to the hospital to see Trammell. 'It meant so much to me,' he told me later, 'to see him one more time.'

"I don't think Bear ever wanted to quit coaching. He had to because of his health, and he believed that his players deserved better coaching than he was able to give them. I used to ask him, 'Why don't you quit? What more can you accomplish?'

"He'd say, 'Quit? I'd croak in a week.'"

At the end of the 1982 season, Bryant announced his retirement, then coached his last game on December 29 — a victory over Illinois in the Liberty Bowl. Less than a month later, at 69, he died of a heart attack.

*Bear Bryant's players were totally enraptured
by him. He didn't coach football, he
coached people.*

PAGES 86–87.
*Before each game, Bryant penned reminders to
himself and kept them rolled up in his hands
on the sidelines.*

April 8, 1974.
Atlanta Stadium.
Fourth inning.
9:07 P.M.

Hank Aaron was guessing fastball. He had already taken Al Downing's first pitch for a ball, but something was telling him the next one would be his. And he was right. The Los Angeles Dodgers' pitcher fired a fastball over the middle of the plate. It was high, higher than Downing had intended, and Aaron swung at the pitch with a coiled flick of his wrists. In an instant, 53,775 fans stood as one, following the ball as it sailed through the rain that was just beginning to fall.

The Dodgers' outfielder, Bill Buckner, raced towards the 385-foot mark in left centerfield, then draped himself atop the fence trying to snare the ball—but it landed ten feet beyond his grasp. "At first, I thought I had a chance to catch it," Buckner said later. "My second thought was to go over the fence after it."

That privilege belonged instead to reliever Tom House, who caught the ball in the Braves' bullpen. House then scaled the fence and ran to home plate to present Aaron with the ball, a ball that was destined for a place in the Hall of Fame.

Aaron now owned a little piece of history—a home run unlike any that had come before it, a home run that had broken Babe Ruth's career record.

Home run No. 715.

Hank Aaron now owns a little piece of history—a home run that broke Babe Ruth's career record.

ERIC HEIDEN

First, he took the 500-meter sprint, then the 1,000, the 1,500, and the 5,000. No man had ever won five individual gold medals, but Eric Heiden looked all but invincible as he stood poised to race over 10,000 meters on a cold, gray morning at the 1980 Winter Olympics in Lake Placid, New York.

The 10,000-meter race is speed skating's version of the marathon, a grueling test of stamina and will, and Heiden knew he could forget about the races that had come before this one. He would need to call on everything his 6 foot 1 inch, 185-pound body had to give, and maybe more.

Heiden raced in the second pair with Viktor Leskin of the Soviet Union. After lagging behind the Russian early in the race, Heiden glided into the lead, legs churning, right arm swinging, and the left arm held behind him for balance. His golden racing suit seemed to shimmer even under clouds as he approached the last two laps. No doubt about it. He was skating at a world-record clip—and turning a normally dull race into a thrilling exhibition of athletic prowess.

When Heiden's time of 14:28.13 was announced, the spectators erupted in delirious applause. He had bettered the world record by more than 6 seconds, knocking an astonishing 22 seconds off the old Olympic record—and finishing 8 seconds ahead of Dutch silver medalist Piet Kleine. A fifth gold medal was his, and later he asked, heck, what's all the fuss? "They just don't really mean that much to me," he said. "They'll probably sit where all the rest of my trophies are—in my mom's dresser. Just giving 100 percent and knowing you did the best you can, that's what's important."

O.J. SIMPSON

He ran with the grace and balance of a great dancer, cutting, faking, and changing speeds with hints of music in every gesture, then bursting into daylight and whistling past hapless defenders. In 1973, when O.J. Simpson practiced his art with the Buffalo Bills, he took an entire pro football season and made it his own. It came down to December 16 and a game against the New York Jets in Shea Stadium. Snow was falling, and O.J. glided across the field with an eerie elegance. There was 4:26 remaining in the first quarter when Simpson churned through the left side of his line for six yards—and broke Jim Brown's NFL single-season rushing record of 1,863 yards.

The referee stopped the game and ceremoniously returned the ball to O.J., who deposited it for safekeeping on the sidelines. When he got back to the huddle, his teammates chanted, "More, Juice, more. Let's get more."

There *was* much more. As the Bills sensed Simpson drawing close to the unthinkable distance of 2,000 yards, they paved the way with crushing blocks, and O.J. displayed his full repertory of dancing steps. Then, with 5:56 left in the game, Simpson blew over left guard for seven yards—and the Bills stormed onto the field and hoisted O.J. onto their shoulders. They carried him from the field as 47,740 shivering fans stood to applaud the season's hero.

O.J. had rushed for 2,003 yards.

There was no need for more.

O.J. Simpson glided along the field with eerie elegance. In 1973, he glided for 2,003 yards.

PAGES 96–97.
In two years at USC, O.J. (32) rushed for more than 3,500 yards and was voted the Heisman Trophy in 1968.

PAGES 98–99.
When Simpson broke Brown's single-season rushing record of 1,863 yards, the referee shook his hand.

PAGES 100–101.
When Simpson went over the 2,000-yard mark, 47,740 shivering fans in Shea Stadium stood to applaud him.

JOE DIMAGGIO

The words are endless, describing his grace in the outfield and detailing his seemingly indestructible 56-game hitting streak. He was celebrated in song, picked clean by gossip columnists when he married Marilyn Monroe, and revered by Hemingway's fisherman in *The Old Man and the Sea*.

Of all the words written about Joe DiMaggio, however, the best appeared in the January 1966 issue of *Esquire* magazine. The writer was Gay Talese, and the following anecdote about Joe's marriage to Marilyn is a classic:

"He was 39, she was 27. They had been married in January of that year, 1954, despite disharmony in temperament and time: he was tired of publicity, she was thriving on it; he was intolerant of tardiness, she was always late. During their honeymoon in Tokyo an American general had introduced himself and asked if, as a patriotic gesture, she would visit the troops in Korea. She looked at Joe. 'It's your honeymoon,' he said, shrugging, 'go ahead if you want to.'

"She appeared on ten occasions before 100,000 servicemen, and when she returned she said, 'It was so wonderful, Joe. You never heard such cheering.'

'Yes I have,' he said."

Joe DiMaggio hit safely in 56 straight games—a major league record he established in 1941.

ROGER STAUBACH

"I was between classes and had gone back to my room," Roger Staubach said, recalling his junior year at the U.S. Naval Academy. "I was stretched out on my bed, trying to get some rest, when I heard a commotion in the hall. I got up to see what was going on, and some guys told me that President Kennedy had been shot. I was in a state of shock all day. At the practice field, that was all we could talk about. Our team felt close to him. He had visited us at Quonset Point in Rhode Island, where we trained in the summer before classes started, and he had tossed the coin at the last Army-Navy game. And, of course, he had served in the Navy during World War II.

"Our coach, Wayne Hardin, looked like he had been crying. He told us that he didn't know what would happen to the Army game, but that the afternoon practice was canceled. We knelt and said some prayers, and then we left. There was a memorial service that night, and all the banners for the Army game were torn down. It wasn't until the next Tuesday that we were told that the game would be delayed a week and would be played in President Kennedy's memory at the request of his family. That same day, I got some other news: I had won the Heisman Trophy. I was certainly proud to get it, but I felt no joy. The president's death had really gotten to me.

"At the game that year, I'll never forget how the presidential boxes on either side of the field were empty and draped in black rosettes. The president was supposed to attend the game, and you could practically feel his absence. We beat Army and got invited to the Cotton Bowl to play Texas, which was ranked No. 1 in the country. It was a great opportunity for us, but it was in Dallas. I remember thinking I'd prefer playing anywhere else in the world. I hated Dallas. It had become a symbol of so much sadness and pain to me. I never dreamed that I'd one day make my home there, and would end up loving the city and its people."

Less than a week after President Kennedy was shot, Staubach was named winner of the Heisman Trophy.

SECRETARIAT

"What I remember most vividly about that Belmont Stakes afternoon in 1973 was that instant on the backstretch when Secretariat, bounding along free on the lead, like a stag across a clearing, raced in the sun past the three-quarter pole," *Sports Illustrated*'s Bill Nack said. "I instinctively glanced at the teletimer on the infield tote board and saw it flash its astounding message: 1:09 4/5 minutes! I froze, and then cursed the rider, Ron Turcotte, muttering to myself, 'This is insane! What in the hell does Turcotte think he's doing?'

"The teletimer's message was that Secretariat, only half-way through the Belmont, was already running as fast as horses run. By almost a full second, he had just run the fastest three quarters of a mile in Belmont history. How could he keep it up? I had more riding on Secretariat than anyone at Belmont Park that day. I had been hanging around the horse for a year, filling notebooks, and I had contracted to write a book in the event he were to win the Triple Crown. He had already won history's fastest Kentucky Derby, then took the Preakness, and now all he had to do was win the Belmont to become the first horse since Citation (1948) to sweep the Triple Crown. Twenty-five years!

"Sweeping past the three-quarter pole, Secretariat began opening his lead—to 5 lengths, to 10, to 15, to 18. Turning for home, he was in front by 20. By the eighth pole in mid-stretch, after setting so torrid a pace that he had tied the world record for 9 furlongs and fractured the Belmont Park record for 10, he was in front by 25 lengths. Pandemonium broke loose. Normally sedate patrons of Belmont's Turf and Field Club abandoned all decorum and climbed up on tables to watch. Reporters in the press box started pounding each other on the back. Then, there he was, widening his lead to 31 lengths at the wire and breaking the Belmont Stakes 12-furlong record by almost 3 full seconds.

"In one incredibly audacious stroke, Secretariat had turned what was to be a coronation, a mere crowning of equine greatness, into one of the most moving, memorable spectacles in the history of sport."

*On his way to winning the 1973 Triple Crown,
Secretariat captured the Belmont Stakes by
31 lengths.*

PAGES 120–121.
*In the Preakness Stakes, Secretariat took the
lead at the half-mile pole and streaked home
in 1:54 2/5.*

MICKEY MANTLE

"I'm in a taxi, trying to get to Yankee Stadium. I'm late, and I've got my uniform on. But when I get there the guard won't let me in. He doesn't recognize me. So I find this hole in the fence, and I'm trying to crawl through it, you know? But I can only get my head in. I can see Billy and Whitey and Yogi and Casey. And I can hear the announcer: 'Now batting . . . number 7 . . . Mickey Mantle.' But I can't get through the hole. That's when I wake up. My palms are all sweaty."

Mickey Mantle has this dream almost every night. That's what he told Diane K. Shah in the summer of 1979. Now a columnist for the *Los Angeles Herald-Examiner,* Shah was then on a freelance assignment for *New York* magazine, working on a profile of Mantle as he sat out his eleventh season in retirement. "There are some things one should never attempt in life, not ever—such as searching out your childhood hero," Shah said. "Mickey Mantle was mine. I grew up with his pictures taped to my bedroom walls, and for a number of years, until I went away to college, actually, there stood between my bed and the dresser an enormous Jell-O box that revolved on a pole. Mantle's picture was on the back of the box.

"My childhood years coincided with Mantle's best in baseball. Had I been wiser, I would have known to leave my memories and scrapbooks locked in the old wooden cabinet in my room instead of trying to resurrect both years later in a hotel bar in New York. By then, Mantle was almost 48, and it seemed to me that his face had aged too quickly. There was still a youthful quality about him, though, something that recalled his power and speed, and his grace in the outfield. I knew his stats by heart: 536 home runs, 1,509 RBI's, .298 batting average. And I knew all about his injuries and his terrible knees. He had to quit at 36 because of them.

"So there I was with Mantle, my pen poised over my brand new notebook. My first question was one that a hundred writers before me had always asked him: 'How're your legs, Mick?'

" 'Not so nice as yours,' he said, and he grinned like a kid.

"He wasn't particularly hard to talk to. I had heard he was. What got to me was the sadness in him. His life after baseball hadn't been happy. It wasn't that he had to keep food on the table by making public appearances, which he always found awkward and uncomfortable, or that his knees were

In his 18-year career with the Yankees, Mantle
ended up with 536 home runs, 1,509 RBI's
and a .298 average.

40 feet from the pin. He took a long time studying his putt, to make certain he had read the line correctly. He then rapped the ball firmly up the slope and watched it break some 18 inches to the left in a gradual curve and dive into the cup. That birdie put him in a tie with Weiskopf, and when Weiskopf three-putted the sixteenth for a bogey 4, Nicklaus was out in front to stay.

"Nicklaus is unquestionably the best fourth-round golfer there has ever been. Even when he starts the last 18 so many strokes off the pace that his chances seem hopeless, it is not his nature to think for a moment of conceding the tournament to anyone else. He is never more dangerous than at these times, and it takes a stouthearted competitor, such as a Lee Trevino or Tom Watson, to stand up to the threat that Nicklaus poses. For most golfers trying to protect a lead on the last day, there is nothing more rattling than to look up at one of the leaderboards positioned around the course and see that Nicklaus, who has slowly mounted one of his celebrated rushes, has picked up three birdies in a row and, now in full flight, is within striking distance of overtaking them."

According to the experts, Nicklaus just might be the best fourth-round golfer in the history of the game.

PELÉ

Grace. Cunning. Speed. Ball control. An otherworldly sense of anticipation. None of these gifts really explained what made Pelé the king of soccer. He was simply a genius, a marvelous union of brain and sinew whose like may never pass this way again. Loping towards an enemy goal, he could drag the ball from one foot to the other as if it were attached to him, waiting for the precise moment to accelerate, then catching the defense off guard and creating goals out of seemingly ordinary and improbable situations. He could thread a pass to an open teammate, or dribble the ball between a defender's legs. No player ever shot harder or more accurately, and he could soar above taller opponents to "head" the ball with an uncanny instinct for the net.

Born Edson Arantes do Nascimento, Pelé's nickname, like the nicknames of other Brazilian players, didn't mean anything—until its owner made it synonymous with greatness. He was not yet 16 when he played his first professional game for the Santos Club. At 17, he carved the first notch in his legend by leading the Brazilian National Team to victory in the World Cup. His brilliant playing sparked a second and a third World Cup triumph in 1962 and 1970, a feat no other nation has ever accomplished. In 1975, after a brief retirement, he was lured to the United States by the New York Cosmos—and by the challenge of popularizing soccer in this country. Three seasons later, just shy of his thirty-seventh birthday, he retired for good.

In a career that spanned 22 years, Pelé scored 1,281 goals, twice the number of his nearest challenger, an achievement that is roughly equivalent to Hank Aaron having hit 2,000 home runs instead of his record 755. Pelé played in 88 countries and visited with two Popes, five emperors, 10 kings, and 108 other heads of state. More than 75,000 people showed up at Giants Stadium for Pelé's last game, an exhibition between his adopted team, the Cosmos, and his home town, Santos. Playing a half for each team, Pelé scored a goal for the Cosmos in a 1–1 tie. When it was over, he left the field to a thunderous chant that expressed the feelings of countless millions in every corner of the world: "Love! Love! Love!"

Pelé was a nickname, but it didn't mean anything—until its owner made it synonymous with greatness.

OAKLAND A'S

They rumbled in the clubhouse, feuded with their managers, and despised their owner. This was no ordinary team, these Oakland A's, who were never truly happy unless they were unhappy. Somehow they managed to grumble and gripe their way to three straight World Series triumphs—'72, '73, and '74—a feat matched only by the New York Yankees of 1936–39 and 1949–53. Unlike the Yankees, however, the A's relied on a superbly balanced attack rather than pure power. Third baseman Sal Bando was their leader. The starting pitchers, led by Catfish Hunter and Vida Blue, threw with heat and guile, and no team in baseball employed a more effective reliever than Rollie Fingers. Billy North and Herb Washington provided speed, while shortstop Bert Campaneris anchored a sure and confident infield. And when the A's needed someone to clear the bases, they turned to outfielders Reggie Jackson and Joe Rudi.

The jolly green-and-gold gewgaw who owned them, Charles O. Finley, ruled his soap-opera troupe with all the grace and charm of a Scrooge. Once, when asked if he had talked to Finley recently, an Oakland player replied, "No, not at all. Every time I call him, he's out walking his pet rat."

All the laughter soon died in free agency. With new freedom to play out their contracts and offer themselves on the open market, several A's players refused to remain with Finley. To cut his losses, he started trading them before they could walk away. Then, in June 1976, Finley sold Fingers and Rudi to the Boston Red Sox for $2 million and Blue to the Yankees for $1.5 million.

Within 48 hours, however, in an unprecedented action, commissioner Bowie Kuhn vetoed the sales, accusing Finley of trying to wreck his own team. He then set a $400,000 limit on all future transactions to prevent the wealthier clubs from cornering the market on the game's stars. "Kuhn sounds like the village idiot," Finley fumed.

Finley sued, challenging Kuhn's authority to intercede. The decision came down in 1977, when a federal court upheld Kuhn's banning of high-priced player sales. The loss seemed to demoralize Finley. Three years later, he sold the A's to a couple of local businessmen—and muttered something about baseball not having Charley O. to kick around anymore.

Charles O. Finley ruled his green-and-gold soap-opera troupe with the grace and charm of a Scrooge.

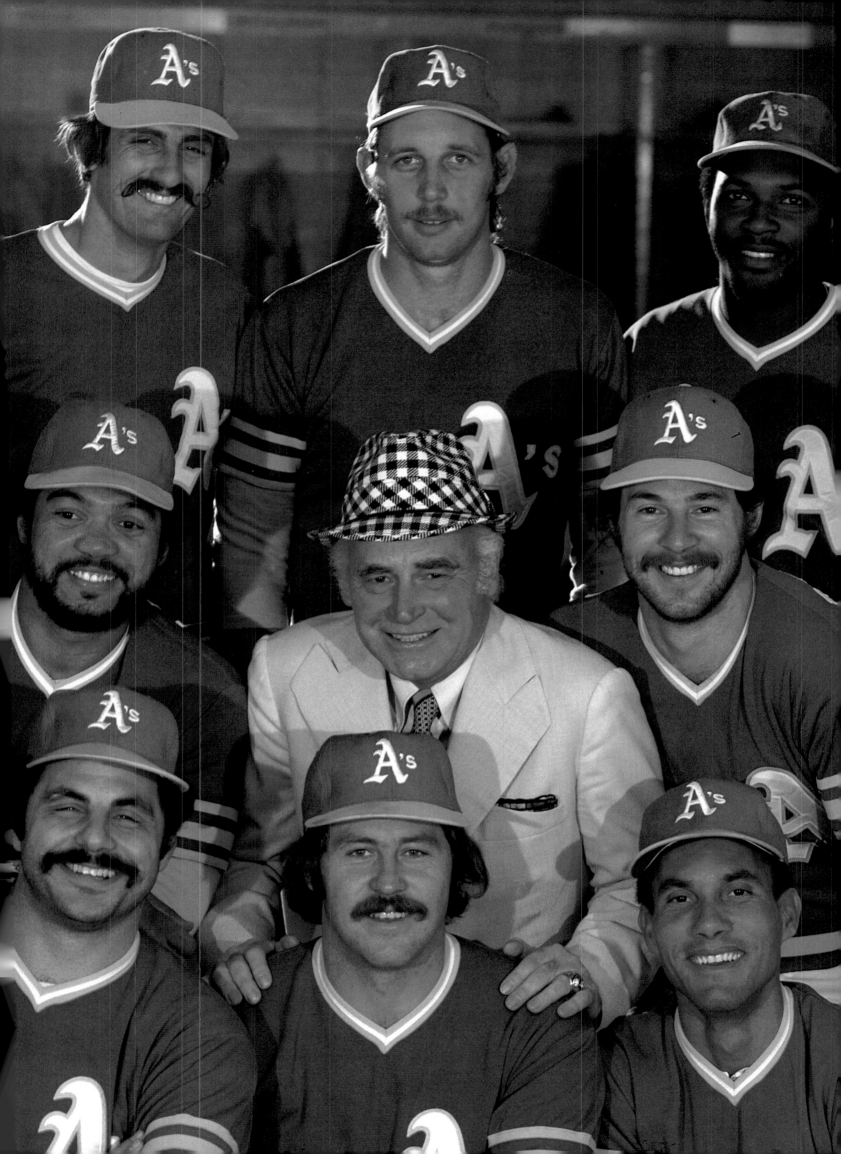

NATE ARCHIBALD

Each summer, Archibald went home again to the South Bronx, never forgetting the kids who could be saved.

Nate (Tiny) Archibald stood a shade above 6 feet, and weighed maybe 160 pounds. He was something to see, darting between giants, flicking passes and left-handed jump shots, hanging suspended on his drives to the hoop. He survived 10 seasons in the NBA, but no matter where he spent his winters playing basketball—in Cincinnati, Omaha, Kansas City, New Jersey, Buffalo, or Boston—he'd always return each summer to the mean streets of his youth. He never forgot the kids who might need him and still could be saved.

"I was raised in the South Bronx, over on 149th Street in the Patterson projects," Archibald said. "One of the earliest things I remember is being told not to eat the rat poison. It was tough. There were a lot of gangs then, like the Schemers, the Suicides, the Black Spades, just beating guys up. Now, it's drugs, and people are dying.

"Two of my brothers got hooked, but they kicked it. A guy named Ralph Hall, a really fine player and my teammate at DeWitt Clinton High School, he was a junkie. One day, I saw him collapse and die on a playground in Harlem. Pee Wee Kirkland, another one. He laughed at the Chicago Bulls when they offered him $30,000, said he could make that much money on the streets. Sure, he could. Pee Wee ended up doing time in a federal penitentiary.

"I worry about the kids, and they know they can trust me because I understand. I'm always there for them, coaching playground teams in the summer leagues. I was raised on strict coaches, so I give 'em hell. Life is full of rules, and the sooner they learn to follow them, the better. It's a shame that a lot of pro players don't go back home to the community and make the kids realize the value of basketball as a means of getting a free education. The players just don't give a damn. I try to give the kids confidence, have them see how it happened for me. A lot of guys were better players than me, but I got good counseling. If some people hadn't told me how to improve my game and my life, I might not have made it. Thank God for my mother, Julia, a good, strong woman. And thank God for basketball."

WAYNE GRETZKY

Even the statistics don't quite sum up Wayne Gretzky. At 23, with five NHL campaigns and one Stanley Cup behind him, he owns single-season records for goals (92 in 1982), assists (125 in 1983), and total points (212 in 1982). There are many, many more, but Gretzky has overwhelmed the records so completely as to render them irrelevant. The center of the Edmonton Oilers, he is by almost unanimous consent the most subtle, artful, and magical player ever to lace on a pair of skates. Ask the all-time greats about the Great Gretzky, and they speak in reverential tones. Take, for example, Montreal's Ken Dryden, the premier goalie of the 1970s, and Chicago's Bobby Hull, the charismatic wing with the blistering slap shot:

"I never realized he was so quick," Dryden said. "Gretzky's got a will-o'-the-wisp quality to the way he skates. There's such a sense of freedom about him."

"I liked to entertain," Hull said. "I knew people wanted to see me take that biscuit and go with it. Wayne's got that same attitude. He thinks of himself as an entertainer. He doesn't want to come off the ice. He comes to play every game. He *likes* to perform."

"Gretzky has an enormous sense of patience," Dryden said. "Everybody has a moment of panic, but Gretzky's comes so much later than that of other players. When he comes down the ice, there's a point when the defenseman thinks: He's going to commit himself one way or the other now. When that moment passes and Gretzky still hasn't committed, the whole rhythm of the game is upset. The defenseman is unprepared for what might come next. It's not an anticlimax. It's *beyond* the climax. And suddenly a player becomes open who wasn't open a moment before."

"He knows where everyone is at all times," Hull said. "I could *kick* in 25 goals a year if I played with Gretzky."

"You can't commit yourself to Gretzky the way you could to other great scorers," Dryden said. "When you can move the puck as well as he can, there's no reason to shoot very often. Which, of course, works to his advantage."

"Hockey needed a shot in the arm when he came along," Hull said. "It needed a champion. People are again relating to hockey as a game of skill, because that's the way Wayne plays."

Hull on Gretzky: "I liked to entertain, and Wayne's got that same attitude. He doesn't want to come off the ice."

He practically owns the British Open, and he has known the euphoria of conquering Augusta's woods and streams and winning the Masters. But put those triumphs aside. Bring up Tom Watson's name from now until they're carpeting courses in artificial turf, and the people who know such things will tell you about the 1982 U.S. Open at Pebble Beach—and the single most memorable shot any of them has ever seen.

Watson wanted desperately to win his first U.S. Open, and he liked his chances as he approached the last two holes on Sunday. Then, just like that, he was in serious trouble. On the seventeenth tee, he put his drive into the deep grass alongside the green. His ball was only 16 feet away from the hole, but the green was hard and fast and sloped downhill. As Watson studied his lie, Jack Nicklaus was already in the scorer's tent with a score good enough to win. He watched Watson on a television monitor and figured his rival would be lucky to get out with a par-3.

Watson, however, wasn't even thinking par. His caddie urged him to play it cautiously, saying, "Get it close."

"Forget it," Watson replied. "I'm going to make it."

Watson bravely opened the blade of his sand wedge and lobbed a soft chip shot onto the green, gambling everything on one sweet stroke. And he won. The ball smacked against the flagstick—and plopped into the cup for a birdie. A mighty roar filled the air, and Watson danced to the tune, waving his club and laughing with tears in his eyes.

"You could hit that chip a hundred times," said Bill Rogers, who was playing with Watson, "and you couldn't get it close to the pin, much less in the hole."

Watson birdied the eighteenth hole to win by two strokes, and moments later he was shaking Nicklaus's hand. "You little sonuvabitch," a smiling Nicklaus told him, "you're something else."

Watson won the 1982 U.S. Open at Pebble Beach with the single most memorable shot many had ever seen.

When his time came, Roberto Clemente died very much as he had lived—trying to give just a little more than anybody else.

He was 38, and it was New Year's Eve, 1972. Clemente was spearheading Puerto Rico's efforts to aid earthquake victims in Managua, Nicaragua. Not satisfied with merely lending his name to the mercy mission, he went along to Managua to supervise the distribution of 26 tons of food and $150,000 in relief money. Moments after takeoff from San Juan, the DC-7 in which Clemente was riding banked left in the darkness—then crashed into the ocean only a mile from shore.

Clemente was an enigmatic man, aloof towards his Pittsburgh teammates and misunderstood by the press. But he was a hero in Puerto Rico, as much for his outspoken expressions of Latin pride as for his wondrous skills. A writer couldn't interview Clemente without hearing his history of aches and pains—tension headaches, nervous stomach, pulled muscles, curved spine, bone chips, and, always, insomnia. When some wondered if his ailments were real or fancied, Clemente shot back: "If a Latin player is sick, they say it is all in his head."

The more he complained, however, the better he played. With his powerful hands, Clemente could line a pitch off his belt buckle or pick it out of the catcher's mitt. A perennial All Star, he won four National League batting titles—and his last hit in his last regular-season game was the 3,000th of his career. In the outfield, Clemente performed with flair and determination, making circus catches on his belly or running headlong into walls and fences; and he could throw out a base runner from improbable distances.

Throughout his 18-year career, Clemente hungered for the recognition he always felt was denied him. "Nobody does anything better than me in baseball," he said prior to the 1971 World Series—and then he hit .414 in seven games against Baltimore.

It seemed only fitting when, shortly after his death, the way was cleared for a special election to induct Clemente into the Hall of Fame, bypassing the usual five-year waiting period for eligibility. Only once before was that rule waived. In December 1939, when he was dying of a nerve disease, Lou Gehrig was elected to the Hall of Fame. No epitaph would have pleased Clemente more.

Shortly after his death, Clemente was inducted into the Hall of Fame when the five-year rule was waived.

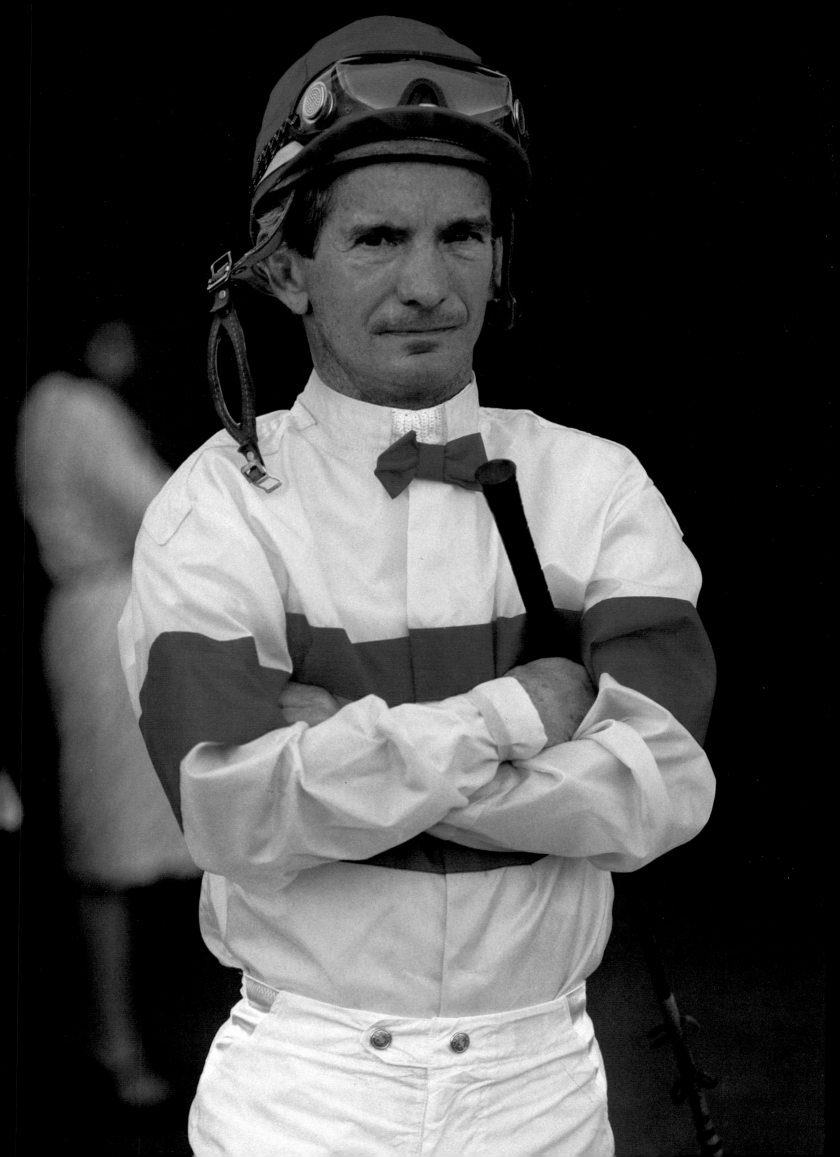

According to *Sports Illustrated*'s Frank Deford, who was there, the 1980 Wimbledon final between Bjorn Borg and John McEnroe was "one of the most extraordinary contests in the annals of sport—or any endeavor in which two men test their wills against one another. For Borg to win his thirty-fifth straight match at Wimbledon and his fifth straight title and to reach a place above all men who have ever played tennis, he had to beat John McEnroe, and he did that by the astounding score of 1–6, 7–5, 6–3, 6–7 (16–18 in the tie-breaker), 8–6.

"Though he was barely 24, no one had ever approached Borg's mark in the championships. Had he won in four sets—as he nearly did—Borg would have been remembered as the juggernaut of the ages, the unbeatable. But by winning the match as he did, he enhanced his reputation, because the character of his performance surpassed the achievement itself. Borg lost seven championship points in the fourth set and finally the set itself. More than that, he lost another seven break points in the deciding set. The last man to lose the Wimbledon final after having a match point in his favor was John Bromwich of Australia in 1948, and those who played against Bromwich thereafter say he was never again the same player. And Borg blew many such chances. And still he triumphed.

"The tie-breaker that decided the fourth set was as excruciating a battle as ever was staged in athletics. It lasted 22 minutes, as long as many sets. Borg had five championship points, McEnroe seven set points, and time and again the man staring down the barrel fired back a winner. The pressure! They won serving, passing, volleying, off both sides, down the line, crosscourt. Neither would yield, neither would swallow hard. Finally, unaccountably, after serving the thirty-fourth point, Borg rushed in and tried to nip a drop volley off a hard McEnroe forehand return, but the ball was hit top-spin and it fell hard on the racket, tumbling off it like a cracked egg.

"As Borg took his position for the fifth set, he thought, 'This is terrible. I'm going to lose.' Borg admitted he thought that. And he thought, 'If you lose a match like this, after

In 1980 at Wimbledon, as he got ready for the fifth set against McEnroe, Borg thought he would blow it.

PAGES 152–153.
Borg won five Wimbledon titles, but he failed to win the U.S. Open, losing four times in the final round.

all those chances, you will not forget it for a long, long time.' It was his serve to start the last set. He lost the first two points. After that, however, he was to serve 29 more times in the match, and he was to win 28 points, the only loser coming at 40–love in game nine. He was inhuman again. But he had been human, so very mortal, and that was important. We already knew the great Borg could beat any opponent. In fact, how much did it really matter, five Wimbledons or four? But that afternoon we found that Borg could not possibly be beaten by himself either. That's why the fifth championship mattered so.

"McEnroe did not only lose, either. Borg had to defeat him. Thus, McEnroe made Borg greater, elevated him for posterity. Louis needed his Schmeling more than the bums-of-the-month, as Ali did his Frazier, Tilden his Johnston. What McEnroe did for Borg with that one match was to lift him above the record books and enroll him among the legends.

"In the final game, at 6–7, McEnroe could not get down for a return chipped to his feet. Nor could he reach quite far enough for a crosscourt forehand. Then, on his eighth championship point, Borg hit a solid backhand crosscourt off a good forehand volley. It whistled home clean. The champion fell to his knees in exultation. Only then did he show any signs of fatigue, in his face, in his eyes. He looked drained, frightened in some way, so different from all those who clamored with joy at what they had just seen of him and of tennis. But Bjorn Borg was the only one who could have seen clearly within himself, and, my God, it must have scared even him to discover how much was really there."

Less than three years later, Borg retired from tournament competition, saying he was burned out. In addition to his five Wimbledon titles, he had won six French Opens, two Italian Opens, two Masters, and one WCT championship. As hard as he tried, though, and as much as he wanted it, he failed to win the U.S. Open, losing four times in the finals.

When Borg fell to his knees in exultation, the crowd clamored with joy at what they had just seen of him.

ORDER NOW FOR 'THE BIG NINE'
FINAL HOME STAND OF THE DODGERS
SEPT. 20-N 21-N 22-D.....PIRATES
SEPT. 24-N 25-N 26-N........METS
SEPT. 27-N 28-N 29-D..PHILLIES
TICKETS AVAILABLE ALL OFFICES
OR BY MAIL--
DODGERS BOX 100 L.A. 51

JIMMY CONNORS

"If you ask Jimmy Connors why New Yorkers like him so much, he'll tell you it's because he spills a little blood out there," columnist Mike Lupica of the New York *Daily News* said. "And he's right. The crowds love him for it, and they love him in a way they've never loved Bjorn Borg or John McEnroe, who's one of their own. What you've got to understand, though, is that Connors wasn't exactly a matinee idol when the U.S. Open was played at the West Side Tennis Club in Forest Hills. The site was too genteel. The romance between Connors and the city didn't blossom until the Open was moved to the raucous National Tennis Center in Flushing, which is hard by a subway station and Shea Stadium. The people who came out to see him there weren't just tennis fans; they were *sports* fans, *New York* sports fans. And they responded to the skinny little middleweight who grew up in St. Louis . . . oops, actually East St. Louis, which is in Illinois and which is the wrong side of the tracks.

"In 1978, the first year the Open came to Flushing, there was a moment when Connors threw back his head and flung up his arms and roared like a New Yorker. He had just hit one of those you-had-to-see-it-to-believe-it running two-fisted backhands against Adriano Panatta, and the ball sizzled past the Italian for a winner down the line. At that instant, the crowd knew Connors would survive the five-setter and triumph—and it roared right back at him.

"In all, Connors has won four Opens in his own inimitable style. He sweats, he grunts, he snarls, he curses, he roars, trying to out-yell New York. And he *tries.* In show biz parlance, he knows how to work a room, and New Yorkers eat it up."

If you ask Connors why New Yorkers like him so much, he'll tell you it's because he spills a little blood.

ARNOLD PALMER

Arnold Palmer joined the pro tour in 1955, and along the way took the staid old game of golf on a merry ride to new heights of popularity. He won one U.S. Open, two British Opens, and four Masters, and he became the first player to reach the one-million-dollar mark in earnings. The money never seemed to matter, though, not to the sport's mavens, weekend duffers, and casual fans. They loved Arnold Palmer for being Arnold Palmer—bold and dashing, relentless and charismatic. Wherever he played, they followed, thousands of them, like an army. Arnie's Army.

When author George Plimpton covered Palmer at his peak, he became a soldier in Arnie's Army. "With his Army behind him, Palmer was like the Great White Knight," Plimpton said. "Golf was being attacked. This sport that had caused so much heartache to the duffers in the Army was about to be conquered. That's the impression you got from the style of the man. The enemy was the course. Balls were butchered. Holes were destroyed. But it was a jolly attack. It was *joie.*

"This Army of Palmer's was an unforgettable phenomenon. Of the various places I've been and of the events I've been fortunate to have been a part—the bog at Watkins Glen during the Grand Prix, the Indy 500, sitting in the bleachers of Wrigley Field for a Chicago Cubs game, the Ali-Frazier fight in Zaire—the Army was the most electric thing I've seen. There's been nothing like it since. It was as if . . . well, rather than Ali having his crazy cadre of hangers-on and sycophants around him, he had 50,000 of them at all times. And because of it, trying to cover Palmer was almost impossible. Sometimes I'd be lucky enough to see the tip of one of his clubs on a backswing. I'm 6 foot 4, but I still couldn't see over the masses. And trying to follow him down the course was not unlike running before the bulls in Pamplona.

"I found this experience one of the most exhilarating a sports enthusiast can have. I was transfixed by the excitement of it. I'd never believed that a golf course or a golf stroke could move me so, but Palmer made golf an art of such excitement. Why? I think a golfing writer named Charles Price put it best. He said that, while walking to a tee or green, Palmer is unlike any golfer in that he climbs onto them, as if clambering into a prize ring."

Plimpton on Arnie's Army: "Trying to follow Palmer down the course was not unlike running before the bulls in Pamplona."

REGGIE JACKSON

Reggie Jackson hit his first big-league home run in an Oakland A's uniform on September 17, 1967. Exactly 17 years later, he hit his five hundredth as a California Angel. In between, for six tumultuous seasons, he was a New York Yankee. His nickname: Mr. October.

Jackson was a larger-than-life presence in pinstripes, a fascinating enigma—mercurial, provocative, egotistical, theatrical, charismatic—who constantly re-created himself to keep everybody guessing and paying attention. The elements were so mixed in him that his strikeouts were almost as electrifying as his home runs. As only the thirteenth player to have hit 500 or more home runs, however, don't expect Jackson to dwell on his strikeouts. But ask him about his most memorable home runs, and he'll instantly recall a cool, crisp October evening in Yankee Stadium.

The year was 1977. Holding a 3–2 lead over the Los Angeles Dodgers, the Yankees needed one more victory to wrap up the World Series. Thanks to Jackson, they got it. His first home run was a classic blow. With a smooth, extended swing, Jackson teed off on a belt-high fastball thrown by Burt Hooton—and sent it into the right field stands. The second one came on an inside pitch by reliever Elias Sosa. Jackson attacked the ball with an awkward, chopping motion, and it too landed in the right field seats. The third homer was a monster. Another reliever, Charlie Hough, threw a knuckleball, low and away, and Jackson drove it 450 feet into the center field bleachers.

Three different pitchers. Three first pitches. Three swings. Three home runs. Not since Babe Ruth had anyone slugged as many home runs in one World Series game. Jackson said he'd never forget the cheers, and how the crowds called his name for all the world to hear.

"REG-GIE! REG-GIE! REG-GIE!"

In 1977, Jackson became the first player since Babe Ruth to hit three home runs in one World Series game.

JOE NAMATH

At 21, Joe Namath was a star, and at 25, a legend. His stunning moment of glory came on January 12, 1969, in Super Bowl III. The New York Jets were 19-point underdogs, but Namath laughed at the odds—and guaranteed all who'd listen that he and his teammates would crush the mighty Baltimore Colts. The final score: 16–7. The winner: the Jets. The hero: Namath. As the architect of a seemingly impossible triumph, he gave instant credibility to the merger between the upstart American Football League and the haughty National Football League.

When Namath was through with professional football, he had thrown for 27,663 yards and 173 touchdowns. Nice numbers, but throw them out. Namath's enduring celebrity transcends football. Along with Muhammad Ali, he was a symbol of a cultural movement. The late '60s and the early '70s were years of compelling social and political upheaval, and Namath's shaggy hair, mustache, white shoes, and sensual lifestyle represented inevitable, triumphant change. He was an antihero who shocked the Establishment by declaring, "I like my Johnny Walker Red and my women blonde."

Years later, Namath quit scotch and switched to vodka, then gave up blondes and married a brunette. His life is simpler now—occasional acting jobs, television commercials, that sort of thing—but it's a good bet that glamour and style will always be with him. And for those who'd like to remember the halcyon days of yore, here's a story. Namath and Jets teammate Ed Marinaro were sitting in a popular New York saloon, drinking into the shank of the night. When Namath was ready to leave, he nodded towards a woman at a nearby table and informed Marinaro that he intended to take her home with him. Incredulously, Marinaro responded, "Joe, you were my idol all through college, and I just can't imagine you leaving a bar with anything less than a 10. And, to be honest, Joe, this woman, even on her best nights, is a 6."

Namath said, "Eddie, it's three in the morning, and Miss America just ain't coming in."

When Namath was through with professional football, he had thrown for 27,663 yards and 173 touchdowns.

PAGES 170–171.
With his shaggy hair, mustache, white shoes and sensual lifestyle, Namath represented triumphant change.

PAGES 172–173.
Years later, Joe Willie quit scotch and switched to vodka, then gave up blondes and married a brunette.

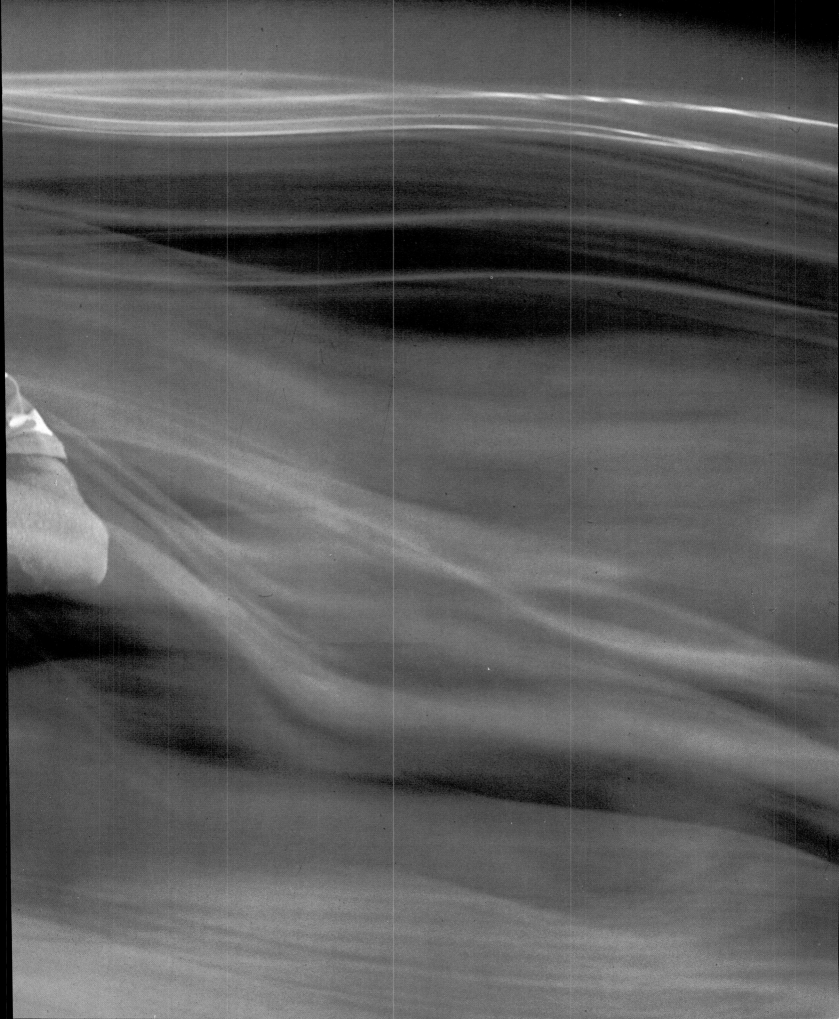

CASEY STENGEL

Casey Stengel was born on July 30, 1890, and died on September 29, 1975. In between, he put in 14 years in major-league outfields, then achieved enduring celebrity as manager of the mighty New York Yankees (1949–60, 10 pennants, 7 World Series) and the lowly New York Mets (1962–65, 175 wins, 404 losses). He was shrewd, combative, forthright, obstinate — and, above all, a brilliant manipulator of players. He talked nonstop, and what he said became known as Stengelese. To some, it was incomprehensible blabber; to others, an amusing blend of sharp observations, pungent non sequiturs, and stream-of-consciousness diversions.

The latter version of Stengelese is favored by those who knew him best. According to them, if you listened carefully and stuck with Stengel long enough, he often made damn good sense. Stengelese reached legendary heights on July 9, 1958, when Casey testified before the Senate Subcommittee on Antitrust and Monopoly in Washington. Baseball was seeking legislation that went beyond its long-held antitrust exemption, and the senators had invited a number of the game's personalities to testify.

SENATOR ESTES KEFAUVER: Mr. Stengel, you are the manager of the New York Yankees. Will you give us very briefly your background and your views about this legislation?

STENGEL: Well, I started in professional baseball in 1910. . . . I entered in the minor leagues with Kansas City. I played as low as Class D ball, which was at Shelbyville, Kentucky, and also Class C ball and Class A ball, and I have advanced in baseball as a ballplayer. I had many years that I was not so successful as a ballplayer, as it is a game of skill. And then I was no doubt discharged by baseball in which I had to go back to the minor leagues as a manager, and after being in the minor leagues as a manager, I became a major league manager in several cities and was discharged, we call it discharged because there is no question I had to leave.

And I returned to the minor leagues at Milwaukee, Kansas City, and Oakland, California, and then returned to the major leagues. In the last 10 years, naturally, with the New York Yankees, the New York Yankees have had tremendous success, and while I am not a ballplayer who does the work, I have no doubt worked for a ball club that is very capable in the office.

I have been up and down the ladder. I know there are

Between 1949 and 1960, Stengel managed the New York Yankees to 10 pennants and 7 World Series triumphs.

Between 1962 and 1965, Stengel managed the New York Mets to a dismal record of 175 wins and 404 losses.

some things in baseball 35 to 50 years ago that are better now than they were in those days. In those days, my goodness, you could not transfer a ball club in the minor leagues, Class D, Class C ball, Class A ball. How could you transfer a ball club when you did not have a highway? How could you transfer a ball club when the railroads then would take you to a town, you get off, and then you had to wait and sit up five hours to go to another ball club?

How could you run baseball then without night ball? You had to have night ball to improve the proceeds, to pay larger salaries, and I went to work, the first year I received $135 a month. I thought that was amazing. I had to put away enough money to go to dental college. I found out it was not better in dentistry. I stayed in baseball. Any other questions you would like to ask me?

KEFAUVER: Mr. Stengel, are you prepared to answer particularly why baseball wants this bill passed?

STENGEL: Well, I would have to say at the present time, I think that baseball has advanced in this respect for the player help. That is an amazing statement for me to make, because you can retire with an annuity at 50, and what organization in America allows you to retire at 50 and receive money?

Now the second thing about baseball that I think is very interesting to the public or to all of us is that it is the owner's fault if he does not improve his club, along with the officials in the ball club and the players. Now what causes that . . . ?

KEFAUVER: Mr. Stengel, I am not sure that I made my question clear.

STENGEL: Yes, sir. Well, that is all right. I am not sure I'm going to answer yours perfectly, either.

Stengel testified for 45 minutes, and much of what he was trying to say was drowned in laughter. When Stengel was through, Kefauver called on Mickey Mantle, the Yankees' popular center fielder.

KEFAUVER: Mr. Mantle, do you have any observations with reference to the applicability of the antitrust laws to baseball?

MANTLE: My views are just about the same as Casey's.

PAGES 178–179.
According to those who knew him best, if you listened carefully and stuck with him, Stengel made good sense.

BILL JOHNSON

He was a 23-year-old Californian whose skiing style dismayed the purists and whose brash personality offended them. When other downhill racers dismissed Mount Bjelasnica in Sarajevo, Yugoslavia, as a cruise course, Bill Johnson laughed in their faces, then spit out his words like fists: "I can go straight faster than anybody. It takes a lot of guts to go out there and throw yourself down the mountain." He wouldn't shut up. "I don't know why the others bothered to show up. They might as well give me the gold medal right now. I've got some knees knocking around here. As I see it, there's going to be a helluva fight for second place. If I have a good run, nobody stands a chance."

Squeezing every ounce of speed out of his flaming red skis, Johnson kept his mouth closed long enough to roar down the 1.9-mile run in 1 minute 45.59 seconds—and became the first American man ever to win an Olympic gold medal in an Alpine event. Later, in response to a question about what the gold medal meant to him, Johnson blurted out a single word that was instantly immortalized as the most famous quote of the 1984 Winter Olympics.

"Millions!"

At the 1984 Winter Olympics, Johnson became the first American man to win a gold medal in skiing.

STEVE CAUTHEN

Steve Cauthen left Walton, Kentucky, and arrived in New York when he was only 16, and he made hard-bitten horse players sputter in disbelief. Standing barely taller than 5 feet and weighing 95 pounds, he had a baby's face and a man's brain. The kid, they called him, and they marveled at his clocklike sense of pace and his seat and balance. Even under the most frenetic conditions, the kid's back remained parallel to the ground and his head stayed icily still. "You could serve drinks on the kid's back at the eighth pole," they said, "and not spill a drop before the wire."

In the kid's second year as a jockey, his mounts earned a record $6,151,750. Then came Affirmed, a splendid chestnut colt with a heart as big as his stride. Affirmed was every bit as tenacious as the kid who rode him—and together they won the 1978 Triple Crown. Each race was a revelation, a *mano-a-mano* confrontation between Affirmed and a gallant archrival named Alydar. First, the Kentucky Derby, then the Preakness Stakes and the Belmont Stakes, and each time the kid held on brilliantly and steered Affirmed to a heart-stopping, split-second victory over Alydar. How much better could the kid get?

The answer came all too swiftly. That summer, the kid suffered a terrible spill at Saratoga. After a rough autumn in New York, he endured a nightmarish winter in California, including a losing streak of 110 races. Finally, trainer Laz Barrera and owner Lou Wolfson took him off the champion Affirmed. Some horsemen took the kid for an 18-year-old has-been, but he kept his head about him. He went to England, determined to make a fresh start. He grew a couple of inches, gained some weight and worked hard to master the weird geography and style of horse-racing in a foreign land. In his sixth season of campaigning abroad, he became the first American since 1913 to win the jockey championship of Britain—and the youngest to accomplish the feat since 1946.

The kid was 24, and he had become a man.

Cauthen rode Affirmed to heart-stopping, split-second wins over Alydar to take the 1978 Triple Crown.

PAGES 184–185.
"You could serve drinks on the kid's back at the eighth pole and not spill a drop before the wire."

TOM SEAVER

As he approached the 1985 season, Tom Seaver needed only 12 victories to join the exclusive club of 300-game winners. Throughout his long career—first with the New York Mets, then the Cincinnati Reds, the Mets again, and the Chicago White Sox—Seaver faced few sluggers more feared than Willie Stargell of the Pittsburgh Pirates. Now retired, Stargell recalled, "Tom had intelligence and character. Combine those two virtues with his ability, his stubbornness and his self-confidence, and you've got one helluva competitor. I looked forward to facing him. It was like Ali and Frazier. We brought out the best in each other. I can't tell you how good it made me feel just to stand at the plate and try to beat him.

"When Tom was in the groove—mentally as well as physically—nobody was going to hit him. I remember one time he was behind in the count. I never felt better. He was meat, my meat. I was thinking fastball, a curve or a slider. It could've been up and in or low and away. I was ready. So what does he do? He throws me a batting practice fastball, as big as the moon, and I took it for a strike. Just stared at it in amazement. It was the only pitch I wasn't looking for. The next day, I asked him, 'How in hell could you throw me that kind of pitch?' He said, 'You looked so intense up there, so damned sure of yourself, I figured I'd catch you by surprise.'

"I had my moments, too. One time in Pittsburgh, he tried to come inside on me, and he hit my wrist. The trainer tried to take me out of the game, but I wanted one more crack at Tom. Next time up, I knew he'd try to come in tight again. A guy like Tom doesn't back off. I waited on him, and sure enough, he came inside—and I smacked the pitch into the seats.

"Tom and I really went at it. I liked his style, wasting no time, throwing in a hurry, always challenging you. I enjoyed every minute of it. When I retired I told Tom, 'I'm glad I had the opportunity to compete against you. I really love you for it.' "

By the way, Stargell tagged Seaver for seven doubles, four triples and eight home runs—a glittering .547 slugging percentage. Overall, however, Seaver held Stargell to a .242 batting average, well below his .282 lifetime figure.

Call it a draw.

PAGES 188–189.
Stargell on Seaver: "I liked his style, wasting no time, throwing in a hurry, always challenging me."

WILT CHAMBERLAIN

There were 10 minutes remaining in the game between the second-place Philadelphia Warriors and the last-place New York Knicks when Wilt Chamberlain slammed in a rebound for his 75th point, breaking his own NBA record. Five minutes later, Al Attles, who hadn't missed a shot all night, ignored an easy lay-up and lobbed the ball to Chamberlain. The 7 foot 2 inch center reached high in the air, snared the ball, rattled the hoop—and scored his 89th point.

It was a meaningless game, played on a neutral court in Hershey, Pennsylvania, but Chamberlain and his teammates were determined to turn the evening of March 2, 1962, into a historic occasion. The Knicks had other ideas. Hoping to avoid the embarrassment of being the first pro team to allow a single player 100 points, the Knicks began to stall. For two minutes, Chamberlain was scoreless—and then Warriors' coach Frank McGuire figured out a strategy to ruin the stall. The frantic Knicks collapsed around Chamberlain, but a spinning jump shot gave him his 96th point.

York Larese then stole the ball, lofted a pass to Chamberlain, and watched his teammate dunk the ball. He had 98 points. One minute and 19 seconds were left in the game. The Knicks stalled again, but eventually shot and missed. The Warriors grabbed the rebound. With the clock running out, Joe Ruklie fed Chamberlain, who fired and missed. He grabbed his own rebound and missed again—but the Warriors outscrambled the Knicks for the ball. The seconds were ticking away when Ruklie spotted Chamberlain near the hoop and tossed a pass above the rim. In one sweeping motion, Chamberlain soared, squeezed the ball in his hands and rammed it through the net—100 points!

Twenty years later, Chamberlain recalled: "We won 169–147, but the Knicks didn't care who won or lost. All they cared about was stopping me. I could have scored 150 points if the Knicks had played naturally."

On the night of March 2, 1962, Chamberlain scored an unimaginable 100 points against the New York Knicks.

SUGAR RAY LEONARD

No one who was there in New Orleans or watched the fight on closed-circuit television will ever forget that November night in 1980. Constantly on the move, Sugar Ray Leonard humiliated the proud and fearless Roberto Duran, snapping his head with jabs, pounding his body with a rainbow of blows. He slipped most of Duran's punches. He stuck out his chin, inviting Duran to hit it, then peppered him with combinations. Remember the seventh round? Winding up his right arm as if to throw a bolo punch, Leonard suddenly unleashed a wicked jab that caught Duran squarely on the nose. And then it happened! With 16 seconds to go in the eighth round, Duran dropped his hands and surrendered. *"No mas,"* he said. *"No mas."* He wanted no more of Leonard. Raising his arms in triumph, Leonard once again owned the welterweight title that he had lost to Duran only a few months before in Montreal.

Later on, Duran said he had stomach cramps and was unable to go on. Nonsense. Leonard had exposed him, and he quit.

There was no quit in Tommy Hearns, who faced Leonard on September 16, 1981, in Las Vegas. He was lean and mean, and he had a lethal right hand that was supposed to strip Leonard of his heart and his consciousness. Then came the sixth round. Leonard ducked a wild right and countered with a left hook that pulverized Hearns's ribs. It was perhaps the most damaging blow of the fight, but Leonard hesitated— and the moment was lost. Hearns survived, turned from a slugger into a boxer and worked on Leonard's left eye until it was almost swollen shut. After the twelfth round, trainer Angelo Dundee screamed in Leonard's ear, "You're blowing it, kid! You're blowing it! Now go out there and put him away!"

And Leonard did just that. He landed a vicious right to the temple, staggering Hearns, then blew him away through the ropes. Hearns scrambled to his feet. Leonard put him down again with a three-punch combination and then two rights. Hearns got up. It didn't matter. In the fourteenth round, Leonard threw a right to the head and a left hook to the body that drove Hearns against the ropes. Leonard followed, delivering blow after blow—until the referee mercifully came to Hearns's rescue and stopped the carnage.

Two fights, almost a year apart, and they serve as a testament to the brilliance that was Sugar Ray Leonard.

In the fourteenth round, Leonard drove Hearns
against the ropes.

PAGES 194–195.
Duran surrendered, pleading, "No mas, no mas."

Willie Mays was the most electrifying player of his generation, and sometimes it seemed his grace and power would defy time itself. As a shy and hesitant rookie with the New York Giants in 1951, he went hitless in his first 21 times at bat, and he broke down and sobbed in the locker room. The next day, Mays hit a home run off Warren Spahn. He then helped the Giants to their miracle pennant, and after a two-year hitch in the Army, he led his team to triumph over the Cleveland Indians in the 1954 World Series. It was then that Mays made his incredible, over-the-shoulder catch of Vic Wertz's 450-foot shot to the edge of the Polo Grounds bleachers—a catch many still say has no equal.

Mays was worshiped in New York, but when the Giants moved to the coast in 1958, San Francisco fans gave their hearts to other heroes. Mays felt the rejection deeply, and he longed to return where he had started. In the twilight of his career, he got his wish when the Giants traded him to the New York Mets. His magnificent skills had eroded—but there were moments when his childlike exuberance could still summon memories of New York baseball at its most romantic.

Willie, Mickey, and the Duke. Three center fielders. Three Hall of Famers. Who was the best? The question inspired furious debate that spilled out of living rooms and onto the sidewalks of New York. In the end, Mays outdistanced his two rivals with a .302 average, 3,283 hits, 660 home runs, and 1,903 RBI's.

Mickey Mantle of the New York Yankees said, "Willie could beat you a million different ways. I think I had more power. I'd take that big swing, but Willie made contact more often. Who was faster? Well, Willie had healthier legs. Mine were always messed up. I wish I'd taken care of myself like Willie did. I'd have played longer. Funny how things end up. Willie and me are banned from baseball because we work for casinos in Atlantic City. It doesn't seem right, does it?"

According to Duke Snider of the Brooklyn Dodgers, "With Willie, Mickey, and me playing in New York, some newspapers carried a box every day comparing our stats. When I'd see Willie before a game, I'd joke and say, 'Hey, I got you by three RBI's,' and he'd say, 'Yeah, but my average is 10 points higher.' I used to love watching him hit. Being in center field, I had as good a view as anyone—until I had to go running after my pitchers' mistakes. Remember those basket catches of his? Beautiful. Even when he made them on me, I'd have to admire them."

Mays went hitless in his first 21 at bats.

PAGES 198–199.
Mays was worshiped in New York.

STARR, HORNUNG, TAYLOR

In the '60s, when the Green Bay Packers ruled pro football with uncommon purpose, three players eclipsed all the others—and one play in particular formed the backbone of those championship seasons. In the words of the team's coach, the late, great Vince Lombardi: "There are many great quarterbacks, and I don't mean to be disparaging to any of them when I say Bart Starr is the greatest. He's smart and disciplined. He takes command. He's a leader. If we're in this game to win, then he is the best quarterback ever to play because he won the most championships. It's as simple as that.

"We had excellent blocking backs in our halfback, Paul Hornung, and our fullback, Jim Taylor. In the middle of the field, Hornung was probably only a little better than the average player. Inside the 20-yard line, that was another story. Nobody in pro football was greater. He smelled the goal line. But when I say that Hornung may have been the best all-around back ever to play football, it's because his blocking had a lot to do with it.

"Jim Taylor would have been the best back if they had let him carry the ball while he was blocking. But he still was excellent. Sometimes, when he broke into the secondary, he would look for those defensive guys just so he could sting 'em a little. He relished the contact. I think Jim Taylor was impervious to pain.

"These were the men in the driver's seat when we used the bread-and-butter play in our offensive category—the power sweep, as we called it. The actual number of that play was 49, which was run to the right or strong side. The reciprocal of it was 28, which was run to the left or weak side. This was the play we felt that every defense we faced had to stop.

"In simplest terms, Jimmy Taylor's job was to attack the defensive end, go directly at him, take him out. By this time, the guards had started to pull, and Paul Hornung was moving to his right and running parallel to the line of scrimmage just as hard and as fast as he could. As soon as Paul took the hand-off from Bart Starr, he had to 'control' his running; that is, he had to permit his teammates to execute their blocks. He couldn't get ahead of them. In particular, he had to read

Lombardi on Starr: "He is the best quarterback ever to play because he won the most championships."

PAGES 202–203.
Lombardi on Taylor: "When he broke into the secondary, he would look for the defensive guys just so he could sting 'em."

the block of his tight end on the linebacker—and quickly decide whether to go inside or outside of that block. That was the beauty of the power sweep. It really had two holes. That's what we called running to daylight.

"Now, not all sweeps were run to the right with Hornung carrying the ball. Remember, there was the 28 play, the weakside sweep with Taylor as the ball carrier and Hornung as the lead blocker. Of course, numerous blocking variations could develop as the play unfolded, but essentially there was nothing spectacular about the power sweep. It was simply a yard gainer. And it fit my philosophy of winning football. I didn't want to hear about trick plays and magic formations. If you blocked better, tackled better, ran better, and passed better, then you were a winner in the game of football."

Lombardi on Hornung: "Inside the 20-yard line, nobody in pro football was greater. He smelled the goal line."

JULIUS ERVING

He left the University of Massachusetts after his sophomore year, then played with the Virginia Squires and the New York Nets in a new league before joining the establishment as a Philadelphia 76er. That was the itinerary—but it doesn't begin to describe the journey that Julius Erving turned into a magical mystery tour. One who went along for the ride was columnist Tony Kornheiser of the *Washington Post,* and he tried to explain the importance of being Julius Erving to his three-year-old daughter.

"This way, Elizabeth, here's someone I want you to see. The man in this picture here, he's the most spectacular player your Daddy ever saw. His name is Julius Erving, but most people called him 'Dr. J,' or just 'Doc,' because of the way he operated on the court. Before you were born he played in the American Basketball Association. A lot of fabulous players spent time in the ABA. Players like Rick Barry, Connie Hawkins, Billy Cunningham, George Gervin, and Moses Malone. But there was nobody quite like the Doc. Looking back, I think it's fair to say that the reason there isn't an ABA anymore is because of Erving; the NBA agreed to a merger because it ultimately recognized that no matter how many major markets it had tied up, and no matter how many superstars it advertised, this guy was the hottest thing since sliced bread and the public demanded to see him. Erving was heir to Elgin Baylor and progenitor of Michael Jordan—the Son between the Father and the Holy Ghost of Hang Time. There has never been anyone better in the open court, never anyone who could thrill a crowd, who could bring people to their feet as spontaneously as Doctor J. When I watched him I often thought he didn't pattern his game after other players as much as after distant eagles. To see him soar and swoop was to appreciate flight and its awesome possibilities. The excitement started as soon as he got his huge hands on the ball. From midcourt, it took him only three dribbles to reach the foul line and rise into the air, lean and mean like a bullet, evading all things in his path to the hoop, finally jamming the ball through the net with contemptuous fury. I always hoped that just once he would lift off and go over the glass, out of the arena, and disappear into space."

In 1983, flying high over the rest of the NBA, Dr. J led the Philadelphia 76ers to the league championship.

Martina Navratilova

She is the athlete as machine—efficient, durable, predictable. It's not an image that Martina Navratilova is entirely comfortable with, and she bristles at suggestions that she has turned women's tennis into a boring tea party where the hostess has the last word. Yet such suggestions aren't altogether inappropriate. While other female athletes grunt and sweat to express their skills, Martina ripples with barely harnessed power, and her ferocious style of play makes it seem as though she is "beating up all those innocent young girls," as she wryly puts it.

No wonder then that each new triumph has prompted speculation as to how one might beat her. Some have proposed driving over her with a truck. Others have advised playing her like a man—meaning serve and volley and try to beat her at her own muscular game. "They can do all the things I do," Martina said. "They can get out there and run on the track. They can lift weights. They can play basketball, full court, one on one, for an hour to get in shape. They can eat the right foods and practice three or four hours a day. There is not anything that I do that anybody else cannot do."

Once plagued by a delicate psyche, Martina conquered the emotional turmoil of her defection from Czechoslovakia and reversed her reputation for blowing the big matches. Wimbledon became her private playground, and the cognoscenti started to compare her to the all-timers—Suzanne Lenglen, Helen Wills Moody, Mo Connolly, Billie Jean King. This woman's a pure player, they said, a natural who's out there on the same artistic plane as the Magic Johnsons and the Great Gretskys of sport; break down her game, and you won't find a single weakness.

SERVE: Ready to serve, Martina sets her body weight in even balance, poised to shift it all behind her forward thrust. The beauty of her serve is the toss, the ball leaving her hand only after a perfectly straight right arm reaches as high towards the sky as possible. The ball is rarely tossed slightly to the right or left, giving no hint where the serve is going. The forward thrust and the ideal toss make the rest easy—a swift, smooth motion that produces a flat bullet serve, a classic left-hander's slice, or a wicked kicker.

FOREHAND: Martina's loose Eastern grip allows her unequaled versatility. Her topspin forehand is like a sportscar on a hairpin turn, downshifting then accelerating to hold the road. Her backswing starts low and picks up enough speed

The beauty of Martina's serve is the toss, her right arm reaching as high towards the heavens as possible.

to ensure her optimum control over her follow-through. The racquet head winds up on the other side of her neck, while the ball dives deep and hard—a crucial factor in her ability to dominate baseliners.

BACKHAND: Martina's superb footwork is what makes this stroke. She positions her side to the ball, her right leg bent low behind her to propel her from her toes. The left leg is planted firmly in front of her as she whips her arm from a low backswing. At the same time, she tucks her elbow into her bellybutton, ready to come over the ball with a high follow-through for maximum topspin. In perfecting this shot, Martina learned to think of launching a missile. Again, she can hit it flat or with a familiar slice, which is very effective when approaching the net.

VOLLEY: In recent years, no aspect of Martina's game has improved more than her play at net. She credits her former coach, Dr. Renee Richards, who pasted a photo of Billie Jean King's volley on her pupil's refrigerator. Now, the forehand volley has an open racquet face, the elbow tucked in close with just enough shoulder rotation. Martina's momentum forward into the shot supplies all the power she needs. A full swing isn't necessary.

OVERHEAD: Here, Martina uses the same motion as on her serve. Once again, the overriding feature of the shot is her athletic ability. She is quick enough to get back behind the ball and keep it in front of her rather than straining to reach for it. The other advantage of her athletic ability is that she always has both feet off the ground for maximum height, while at the same time keeping her head steady and her eyes focused on the ball. In addition, she hits the shot without tipping off which way she's aiming the ball.

Put them all together, and you've got a player who won 90 of 93 matches in 1982 and 86 of 87 in 1983. The next year, Martina won her fifth Wimbledon title, her second French Open, and her second U.S. Open. In the process, she took a record 76 consecutive matches. Unfortunately, the 77th was a loss to a kid named Helena Sukova in the Australian Open—which deprived her of becoming the first player to win seven straight major tournaments. After the match, nobody doubted Martina when she said, "It hurts, but I'll get over it."

In 1984, rippling with power, Martina won Wimbledon for the fifth time—and a record 76 straight matches.

Joe Frazier was proud and defiant, a fierce warrior who plied his trade the only way he knew how. He sacrificed his face, taking three blows to deliver one, always attacking, accepting the pain and the scars of his profession to get inside and overwhelm his opponent with relentless brutality. He held the heavyweight championship for almost five years, then got knocked out in the second round by George Foreman in January 1973.

Frazier had only one chance to be champ again, and it came against Muhammad Ali in 1975. The fight turned into an intensely personal contest, a savage, unpredictable clash of wills that Frazier would eventually lose. In losing, however, Frazier fought the most gallant fight of his life.

In the weeks before the "Thrilla in Manila," Ali taunted Frazier, calling him a gorilla—and predicting an early knock-out over a washed-up old rival. Frazier responded with an earthy promise of his own: "When Clay hears the knock on the door, he'll forget all that crap he's been saying. He'll remember that inside those four corners, there's not another man like me in the world."

Ali started fast, snapping jabs and straight rights to Frazier's head. By the fifth round, however, Frazier's jack-hammer blows seemed to have Ali paralyzed against the ropes. Frazier owned the middle rounds, his deadly left hooks raising welts on Ali's handsome face. Towards the end of the eleventh round, he looked like he still had more to give—but Ali had somehow managed to reach beneath his agony and alter the course of the fight. Suddenly, Ali began hitting Frazier at will with combinations, closing the challenger's left eye. Frazier was helpless against Ali's right-handed punches—and yet he kept coming. His trainer, Eddie Futch, thought that Frazier might be ahead on points, but he also knew that his fighter was in terrible shape. "Can you see?" Futch asked after the fourteenth round.

Frazier shook his head.

"That's it, then," Futch said. "I'm calling the fight."

"No, no," Frazier pleaded, standing to answer the bell.

"That's all, Joe," Futch said, quietly putting an end to the bloody epic, "that's all."

After the fight, it was left to Ali to pay Frazier his finest tribute. "I'm just happy right now," he said, "that there ain't no more Joe Fraziers to fight."

After the "Thrilla in Manila," Ali said, "I'm just happy right now that there ain't no more Joe Fraziers to fight."

VINCE LOMBARDI

Vince Lombardi was obsessed with excellence and success. The former does not necessarily guarantee the latter, and for many years it seared Lombardi's soul. The son of an immigrant Brooklyn butcher, he was a member of Fordham's "Seven Blocks of Granite" line in the mid-'30s. He held a full-time job as an insurance investigator while attending law school, then coached three sports and taught physics, chemistry, algebra, and Latin in a New Jersey Catholic high school. There was a stint as an assistant at West Point and later with the New York Giants, and Lombardi felt the fear of time running out. He mumbled curses and searched for answers to explain why he couldn't get a break. Was it his ethnicity? His bluntness? His lack of glamour?

Finally, at 46, Lombardi knew redemption. Hired as head coach of the lowly Green Bay Packers in 1959, he would make the most of what was given him. A year earlier, the Packers had won only one game. They won seven of twelve games in Lombardi's first season and a Western Division title in his second. Then, they captured five NFL championships in seven years, as well as the first two Super Bowls. The players he ruled ranged from playboy halfback Paul Hornung and self-effacing quarterback Bart Starr to thoughtful defensive end Willie Davis and violent middle linebacker Ray Nitschke. In Lombardi's eyes, however, they were of one heart and mind, and he demanded they put aside their personal ambitions for the good of the team. In an oft-quoted remark that best reflected Lombardi's concept of esprit de corps, tackle Henry Jordan said, "He treats us all the same. Like dogs."

Lombardi aroused reactions in the extreme. Some blasted him for his authoritarian view of life, while others celebrated him as the embodiment of the American way. Actually, he was neither saint nor sadist, genius nor jackass, Patton nor Mussolini. A basically decent man with strong ties to his religion and his family, he could be loyal and sentimental as well as arrogant and ill-tempered. Above all, however, he was fiercely honest and totally committed to his work.

The secret to Lombardi's success was really no secret at all. He was simply smart enough to reduce an increasingly complex and sophisticated game to its most brutally basic and effective form—and then communicate his precepts and inspire his players with almost fanatical zeal. In 1970, after leaving Green Bay and spending only one year with the

Under Lombardi, the Packers won five NFL championships in seven years—and the first two Super Bowls.

Washington Redskins, Lombardi died swiftly of intestinal cancer. He was 57. Many nominated him for instant canonization. One who did not was the then *New York Times* columnist, Robert Lipsyte, who captured the essence of the Lombardi mystique in a farewell headlined, "Lombardi Without Tears."

In part, Lipsyte wrote, "Lombardi himself once said, 'The answer today seems to be to take things easy. The prevailing sentiment is, if you don't like the rule, break it. I believe freedom has been idealized against order.' His philosophy was criticized in his lifetime by those who felt it not only had no application beyond football, but made football a joyless experience as well. Yet the statistics of his success—and in professional football, at least, winning should be the only thing—and the testimony of players thrilled to learn they were better than they thought they were, secured Lombardi's reputation as one of the game's finest coaches.

"But Lombardi's players did not disregard their injuries and search for new levels of energy and push themselves to be working parts of his whole merely because they were afraid of him or because they were proselytized by his slogans. They bled for Lombardi because he promised them the opportunity to be the best, and because he showed them he had the capability of leading them to success. With the same personality and a lesser intelligence, Lombardi would never have been able to tell men that they had better be 'fired with enthusiasm or you'll be fired with enthusiasm.' They would have dogged it in their grass drills and been happy to be traded away.

"Lombardi did not demand purposeless obedience to inflate his ego or impose discipline to control or attack those who disagreed with him because he felt fearful. He demanded and imposed and attacked because it was part of his vision for success, and it all worked only because he came to his people offering them more than he asked."

In 1970, after leaving Green Bay and spending only one season in Washington, Lombardi died of cancer.

GERRY COONEY

Gerry Cooney had the look of a real-life Rocky, a big, handsome white banger who could lay low a mule with his left hook. That same hook had zapped Ken Norton's head and crushed Ron Lyle's ribs. It was the kind of weapon that wins heavyweight titles, and *Time* magazine posed the undefeated contender with Sylvester Stallone for a cover that suggested life would imitate art. It didn't. When Cooney got his shot against the champion, Larry Holmes, in June of 1982, he was hopelessly outclassed. The richest fight in heavyweight history ended in the thirteenth round, when trainer Victor Valle stepped into the ring and hugged his fighter to stop Holmes from hitting him.

Weeks faded into months, and Cooney wouldn't fight. His first defeat had depressed and humiliated him, he said. It was obvious his emotional scars needed time to heal. Then, when he was ready to return, a succession of injuries spoiled his comeback. Finally, more than two years after his loss to Holmes, Cooney beat a stiff named Phil Brown who didn't fight back. Three months later, he scored a second-round knockout over George Chapin, a hospital technician who handled X rays a lot more deftly than right uppercuts.

Will Cooney ever win the heavyweight championship?

"He could," said Mike Marley, an ABC producer and a prolific boxing writer. "After all, there are now three versions of the championship—the WBC, WBA, and IBF—and the heavyweight division basically stinks. But he'll never be the champion he could've been. Gerry got rich off the Holmes fight, but he never fought for the money. He got into boxing to please and appease his father. Then, when his dad died, Gerry wanted to win the title in his memory. Not only that, but his handlers always made it seem like half the world was depending on him. Late in the Holmes fight, one of his managers, Dennis Rappaport, was screaming, 'Do it for the kids, Gerry!' and 'Do it for America!' and 'Do it for your father!' Nobody ever told Gerry to do it for himself. He never wanted to win the championship for himself. The great fighters have a burning ambition. They're either extremely hungry or extremely self-centered, or both. They go after the title for their own personal gratification. Gerry fought for all the wrong reasons. So, when he lost to Holmes, he couldn't handle it. In his mind, he'd let everybody down. He still feels that way. And now that he's financially secure, he's got even less motivation to fight. It's too bad. He misspent the prime of his career."

In Cooney's case, life did not imitate art.

DALEY THOMPSON

After the first five events in the decathlon, Daley Thompson had built a formidable 114-point lead over archrival Jurgen Hingsen of West Germany. And just before the start of the final event, the 1,500 meters, Hingsen offered his hand to the cheeky, irrepressible Brit in congratulations. Thompson needed a 4:34.8 to break Hingsen's world record of 8,798 points. Seemingly easing up at the end, however, he trudged across the finish line in 4:35, two-tenths of a second — and two points — shy of establishing a new world mark. But he had the Olympic record — and joined Bob Mathias as the only athlete to win two decathlon gold medals.

Raised in London, the son of a Nigerian immigrant and a Scottish mother, Thompson grew up poor and angry, but track offered him the chance to run away from trouble. Few athletes so thoroughly relish the rigors of training and competition as Thompson — and even fewer are able to express their joy in ways that make all around them laugh along. One who shared in the laughter was ABC Sports correspondent Dick Schaap. Schaap followed Thompson closely at both the Moscow and Los Angeles Olympics and noticed a lot of the young Ali in him.

"To watch Daley compete is a privilege," Schaap said. "Only in the young Ali have I ever seen confidence, courage, talent, and physical grace similarly mixed. But, as it once was with Ali, it is even more delightful to watch Daley *exist,* to see him tackle life with zest and a wink. One day, he is handing the medal he just won in the Southern England pole-vaulting championships to my daughter, who, not easily impressed, and then not yet a year old, throws it to the ground. Another day, he is tossing my daughter up in the air and catching her until his powerful arms tire, and he surrenders, admitting fatigue.

"I'll never forget a dinner in Moscow, just before he won his first Olympic decathlon championship, when, without speaking a word of Russian, he charmed a group of Soviet guards into permitting him to violate the entrance and curfew rules at my hotel. 'See you later, alligator,' one Soviet security man called to Daley. And I'll never forget our celebration dinner the night after he won his second Olympic decathlon championship, a dinner capped by a telephone conversation I helped set up between one of Daley's admirers, the actor Jack Nicholson, and one of Nicholson's admirers, Doreen Rayment, the woman who raised Daley after his Scottish

Thompson is able to express his joy in being an athlete in ways that make everybody near him laugh along.

mother refused to encourage him to become an athlete. Nicholson and 'Auntie' Doreen spent some 20 minutes on the phone, discussing track and field, and when she got off, she turned to Daley and said, 'That's the first bloody American I've spoken to who knows what he's talking about.'

"I think of Daley at a party in London, challenging Martina Navratilova to play him in tennis if she'll agree to play left-handed (which, as Daley had forgotten, she always does), and of Daley at a party at Wimbledon, spotting Frank Perdue and, after being told about Perdue's chicken empire in America, marching up to him and inquiring, 'Are you the chicken chap?' I remember, too, falling into Daley's trap when, shortly before the 1984 Games, he said to me, of the decathlon competition, 'Everybody *thinks* they might win, or *hopes* they might win, but there's always one guy who *knows* he's going to win.'

" 'Do you *always* know you're going to win?' I said.

"Daley winked. 'So far so good, Dick,' he said.

"He trapped Hingsen, too. When Hingsen promised the people of West Germany he would bring home a gold medal, Daley said, 'There's two ways he can do that. He can steal mine or enter another event.' And then, of course, Daley backed up his bold words with, arguably, *the* performance of the 1984 Olympics. I'm willing to bet that he will celebrate his thirtieth birthday, in 1988, in Seoul, by becoming the first human to win the Olympic decathlon for a third time."

At the Los Angeles Olympics, Thompson scored 8,797 points, two points shy of setting a new world mark.

TERRY BRADSHAW

Terry Bradshaw was a strapping piece of business, a quarterback who survived numerous concussions and still managed to pass for 27,989 yards and 212 touchdowns in 14 years with the Pittsburgh Steelers. Regal statistics, certainly, but connoisseurs point to the Super Bowls in assessing the real measure of the man.

There were four Super Bowls in all, each ending in a victory, and Bradshaw personally contributed nine touchdown passes. No quarterback had ever thrown more. For the record, here they are: In Super Bowl IX, played in New Orleans, Bradshaw hit tight end Larry Brown with a four-yard dart in the closing minutes of the game—and clinched a 16–6 triumph over the Minnesota Vikings. The following year, in 1976, he threw for two touchdowns, the second soaring 59 yards in the air to wide receiver Lynn Swann, who made an acrobatic catch between two Dallas Cowboys defenders—and scampered into the end zone for a 21–17 victory.

Bradshaw waited three years to appear in his next Super Bowl, then threw four scoring strikes—two to wide receiver John Stallworth and one apiece to Swann and running back Rocky Bleier—to beat the Cowboys again, 35–31. The next year, at the Rose Bowl in Pasadena, Bradshaw hit Swann for a 47-yard touchdown to give his team a 17–13, third-quarter lead over the Los Angeles Rams. Trailing 19–17 in the fourth quarter, however, the Steelers looked to Bradshaw for salvation, and their prayers were answered. Having called "60 prevent, slot hook and go" in the huddle, Bradshaw unleashed a mighty toss—and found Stallworth on the dead run for a 73-yard touchdown. The tide turned, and the Steelers rolled to a 31–19 victory. As for Bradshaw himself, he was named the game's Most Valuable Player for the second year in a row.

Bradshaw threw nine touchdown passes in leading the Pittsburgh Steelers to four Super Bowl championships.

CARL LEWIS

Carl Lewis was a winner, but not a hero. He won the Olympic 100-meter dash in 9.99 seconds and the 200 in 19.80, easily took the long jump with a leap of 28 feet ¼ inch, then cruised to victory as the anchorman in the 4 × 100 relay. His four gold medals in track and field matched Jesse Owens's historic performance in 1936, but that's just about as far as it went. It was supposed to mean so much more. Somewhere along the way, however, Lewis tripped over his own carefully laid plans. He heard boos as well as cheers, took a beating in the press—and left the 1984 Olympic Games in Los Angeles with a somewhat tarnished image.

In his finest hour, Lewis always seemed embroiled in some new controversy. Along with several others, he refused to stay in the Olympic Village. He allowed his manager to drool in public over the prospect of lucrative endorsement contracts—and boast that his client would be as big a star as Michael Jackson. He passed up four attempts to break Bob Beamon's long-jump record of 29 feet 2½ inches, and he passed up post-event interviews as well. The criticism grew louder, and Lewis found himself accused of being arrogant and aloof—and stripping the joy and spontaneity out of the Olympic experience.

"Some people said that everything I did was calculated," Lewis said five months later. "Even after I won the 100-meter dash and I ran to the stands and grabbed a flag to run around the track with, some reporters wrote that this was calculated. Look, I've always been exuberant, maybe even a showboat, and when I grabbed that flag, it was spontaneous. The guy I took it from said later that he thought I was just coming over to shake his hand.

"I don't know why people made a big deal out of me not going for Beamon's record. I said many times before that if I was ahead, I wouldn't try for it. I had run in two 200-meter heats in the morning, and I had a race the next day. I wanted to conserve my energy. I also felt a little sore, here, in my left leg, and I didn't want to risk an injury. The press didn't seem to want to understand. The fans who booed just weren't

Somewhere along the way, Lewis tripped over his own carefully laid plans—and heard boos along with cheers.

PAGES 228–229.
Lewis: "The fans who booed just weren't knowledgeable about track and field. I really believe I was treated unkindly."

knowledgeable about track and field. I really believe I was treated unkindly. Now, I'm talking about some of the press and some of the fans, not everybody. I had been Mr. Olympics since '81, and for the most part it was all on my shoulders. Then, when '84 came, it was like, 'You've gotten us here, now goodbye.'

"I know I didn't have the impact that Jesse Owens had. Jesse was my hero. But, you know, for a lot of people, he wasn't a major, major personality until about five years ago, when people began to recall his exploits in 1936. I mean, he came back from Berlin and the President didn't even shake his hand. President Reagan invited me to the White House, and he talked to me about the 100-meter race. I had the impression he watched it very closely on television. And Nancy, she was great. She hugged me.

"In spite of everything, I've received numerous offers for endorsements, but I've accepted only a few. I'm doing fine financially. I've even gotten a supporting role in a movie. We start shooting in a few months, and I make a statement in it against drugs and the night life. Everything's okay. The Olympics weren't a pleasant experience, but I've learned to cope. I felt I was being consistent and doing what I had done to get me there. You're considered wrong for doing what you think is best. I won the four gold medals I had set out to win. And so I wouldn't have changed anything."

Lewis winning fourth gold medal as anchor of the 4 × 100 relay team: "The Olympics weren't a pleasant experience."

BILL BRADLEY

The son of a well-to-do bank president in Crystal City, Missouri, Bill Bradley began playing basketball when he was nine. Within a few years, he had developed such an intense fascination and love for the game that he willed himself to become a superb player even though he wasn't an exceptional natural athlete. Practice, practice, practice—and more practice. He spent endless hours alone, darting and weaving away from imaginary defenders, flicking passes to phantom teammates, perfecting the quick release of his jump shot and working repetitively on the aspects of his game he felt were weakest. Those who knew him well and observed him closely said his fierce desire for improvement was a matter of self-fulfillment rather than proving himself to others. His coach at Princeton marveled at Bradley's Spartan approach to the game. "I think," Butch van Breda Kolff said, "Bradley is actually happiest when he's denying himself pleasure."

On graduation from Princeton, where he broke almost every Ivy League record there was and established himself as the finest college player in the land, Bradley chose to accept a Rhodes Scholarship over a chance to play professional basketball. Two and a half years later, in December of 1967, Bradley had completed his studies and joined the New York Knicks. The next season, he made the most of his opportunity to become a starter at forward when Cazzie Russell busted his ankle, and the season after that, he played a vital role in his team's first NBA championship. It was Bradley, more than anyone else, who put the flow into the Knicks' attack. He seemed to weave his team into intricate patterns, initiating plays with his constant movement, finding the open man with a deft pass, hitting his soft jumper in game-breaking streaks.

The Knicks won their second championship in 1973, and Bradley played another four seasons. The year after he retired, surprising practically no one, especially teammates who often fantasized about reunions in the White House, Bradley ran for the U.S. Senate from New Jersey—and won handily. Re-elected in 1984, he may yet invite his former teammates to a state dinner.

While it is reasonable to suggest that pro basketball stardom helped launch Bradley's political career, it is wrong to assume that he used the game as a springboard to public office. "I had a number of alternatives after Oxford," he once said, "but I think subconsciously I knew I would come back

At Princeton, Bradley broke every Ivy League record there was—and towered over all other college players.

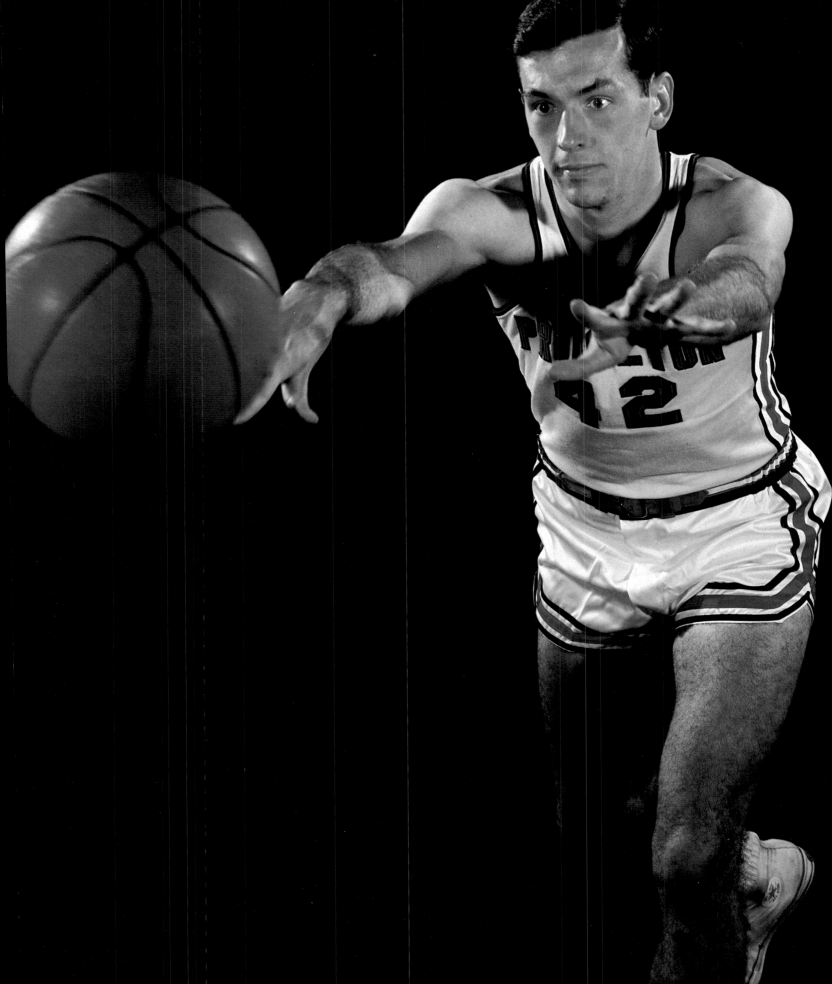

RAY NITSCHKE

"You watch the defensive guys today, and you know they're making more money than you ever did, and they aren't playing the game as they should be," said Ray Nitschke, the Hall of Fame middle linebacker of the Green Bay Packers' glory teams of the 1960s. "They don't know how to tackle. All they worry about is pass defense and blitzing and doing sneaky things. As it is, the guys spend more time running on and off the field than they do playing. They have specialists for everything. To me, they aren't really in the game.

"They used to call Dick Butkus and me 'prototype linebackers.' There's no such thing anymore. Butkus and I were what football players should be—play all four downs and all kinds of plays. Consistent performance, week in and week out. They don't seem hungry now, not every week. Now there's 28 teams. It used to be there were only 12. A lot of the guys around today would have never played back then. The whole game's changed because of all the passing. It's more like a basketball game. Teams used to run the ball, not like the 49ers with those dinky passes all over the place.

"And all the blitzing. You're supposed to use the blitz to cover up your weaknesses. Look at Lawrence Taylor on the Giants. He's an incredible athlete, so fast. But he's like a lineman the way they use him, always blitzing. He gets a lot of spectacular sacks, but he makes a lot of mistakes on pass coverage. With all these great defenses and great defensive players they talk about, there's too much scoring. All those offensive players running all over the place don't mean anything. They got to wind up somewhere, and that's where guys like me and Butkus would be. I saw the Redskins up here last year play the Packers. It was like a tennis match. The final score was something like 49–48. Whoever had the ball last, that's who won.

"That's not football."

Nitschke: "Butkus and I were what players should be—play all four downs and all kinds of plays."

PAGES 242–243.
Nitschke (66) forcing Jim Brown (32) to fumble: "Players don't seem hungry now, not every week."

GORDIE HOWE

Think of Gordie Howe, and numbers dance in your head. He scored his first NHL goal on October 16, 1946, for the Detroit Red Wings and his last on April 11, 1980, for the Hartford Whalers. He retired in 1971, then came back two years later to play with his two sons in the WHA, managing 174 goals and 334 assists in six seasons. Those numbers aren't included in his NHL career records: most seasons (26), most games (1,767), most goals (801), and most points (1,850). He played on four Stanley Cup championship teams, won six scoring titles and was named the League's Most Valuable Player six times. He was a 52-year-old grandfather when he retired for good, and yet he didn't want to let go. "It's not easy to retire," he said. "No one teaches you how. I found that out when I tried it the first time. I'll never again do anything as well as I played hockey, and it's hard to face the rest of your life knowing that. I've got my wife and my boys and my grandchildren, and I'll do my best. I'm no quitter—but I will now quit hockey."

Howe retired at 52, having scored more goals (801) and more points (1,850) than any player in history.

Debbie Armstrong

"I was thinking before the race that I'm really as good as anybody. I thought to myself, 'Well, I know that, so why don't I go out and do it and show everybody else, too?'"

Those words were spoken by Debbie Armstrong, a 20-year-old skier who wasn't given any kind of chance of winning any kind of medal in any kind of race in Sarajevo, Yugoslavia. She had spent two unimposing seasons on the World Cup circuit, and she wasn't exactly a household name even among her high-school classmates in Seattle. There Armstrong was, though, thousands of miles away from home, thinking positive thoughts, and the next thing she knew, she had psyched herself onto the cover of *Sports Illustrated* by executing two inspired charges down the giant slalom course—and winning the first U.S. gold medal of the 1984 Winter Olympics.

In the first run, starting fifteenth, Armstrong skied nearly flawlessly and finished in 1 minute 8.97 seconds. Her time put her in second place, one tenth of a second behind teammate Christin Cooper, who had looked almost unbeatable. Armstrong suddenly looked like a real threat to win a medal, maybe even a gold, because some big names like teammate Tamara McKinney and Switzerland's Erika Hess had experienced difficulty and seemed unable to catch up.

Four days and nights of steady snow had ruined the Alpine racing schedule, forcing the crucial second run to start three and a half hours after the first. Armstrong was wired. Up at the starting gate, she turned to Cooper and babbled, "I'm just going to have fun out there, just have fun, have fun! And when you go down, I want you to relax and just have fun, because I'm going to have fun!" Starting fourth, a rush of adrenaline flowing inside her, Armstrong went rocketing down the slope, negotiating each gate with the aplomb of a veteran. Even so, she seemed to hold something back. Her time was a so-so 1 minute 12.01 seconds—and then she got lucky. Cooper, next on the hill, slipped five gates from the top, and it cost her the gold medal. She ended up in second place, a disappointing four-tenths of a second behind Armstrong.

After the race, the two rivals embraced. There were no sad words from Cooper, only praise for Armstrong—the kid who came out of nowhere and wanted everybody to have a little fun.

Armstrong came out of nowhere, winning a gold medal in the giant slalom and landing on magazine covers.

"The issue date of my first *Sports Illustrated* cover?" photographer Neil Leifer said, repeating the question. "You kidding? November 22, 1961. It was Y.A. Tittle. You know, I've had 152 *Sports Illustrated* covers in my career, but I can remember shooting the first one like it was yesterday.

"By the middle of 1961, my pictures had started to appear fairly regularly in the magazine, but I was still hoping for a cover. The photo editor then was Jerry Astor, and he assigned me to a Washington Redskins home game against the New York Giants. We were doing a story about the Redskins' owner, George Preston Marshall, and why he still had no black players on his team. Demonstrators were supposed to picket the stadium. My job was to cover both Marshall and the demonstrators, not the game—which I intended to shoot on my own time. Before leaving, I stopped by the Nikon shop, and I noticed this new lens—a 500mm, F-5, mirror lens. It was very small, a light, handheld lens. I thought it might be fun to try during the game, and I asked to borrow it. At the time, there were only two such lenses in the world, and the people at Nikon were reluctant to lend me one. Eventually, however, they gave in.

"In Washington, I completed my assignment, then switched to color film for the game. Using Nikon's new lens, I quickly determined two things. When you focused on the players, the background got diffused and made the faces in the crowd look like a multicolored bed of Cheerios. It was also the hardest lens to focus I had yet used. For a variety of technical reasons, I keyed on the quarterbacks. The pictures of Tittle turned out particularly well, and Astor liked them. He then gave me my first cover assignment—a running back named Jimmy Saxton, who played for the University of Texas. I was tremendously excited, and when I got back, I waited anxiously as Astor showed my Saxton pictures at the cover conference. When he came out, there was a big smile on his face. 'Well, Neil,' he said, 'you're going to have back-to-back covers.'

" 'Great,' I said. 'Jimmy Saxton and then who?'

" 'No, no. First, Y.A. Tittle—then Saxton.'

"I couldn't believe it. The editors wanted a cover story on the Giants, and they liked the Tittle stuff I had shot in Washington. And you know something? Looking at that picture all these years later, even taking into account all the advances in photography, it still makes a helluva cover."

*On October 28, 1962, Tittle threw a record
seven touchdown passes against the
Washington Redskins.*

VALERIE BRISCO-HOOKS

Not once, not twice, but three times her tears flowed like jagged streams down her face as she stood atop the victory stand and felt her country's anthem wash over her. She had come a long way. The mean streets of Watts, where she grew up, are only a few minutes by car from the sprawling splendor of the Los Angeles Coliseum. Or a lifetime. There are no guarantees in Watts, even if you can run fast enough to get out.

Just ask Valerie Brisco-Hooks.

One of 10 children, she was 14 when her older brother Robert was shot by a stray bullet on his high school track. A sleek and stylish sprinter, Robert was her favorite, and his death changed her. Previously unwilling in school and undisciplined in sports, she became an interested student, and she ran with all the natural speed that was in her. Robert was her inspiration, and the 200- and 400-meter races were her pleasure. In 1981, she set national junior college records in those events, and then she married Alvin Hooks, who was a wide receiver with the Philadelphia Eagles. They had a son. It was a tough pregnancy, and she gained 40 pounds that stayed with her. "I was really big," she said. "It took me a while to believe in myself and really want to run again."

Her coach, Bobby Kersee of UCLA, never let her give up. He kept going to her house and saying, "Valerie, I know you have it in you," and his words became a part of her training. While she ran, her husband and her mother took care of the baby. Alvin Hooks had been released by the Eagles in 1982, and again by the Los Angeles Express after the 1983 season. Now was Valerie's chance, he knew, and he reacted like the proudest husband in America when she set Olympic records at 200 meters (21.81), 400 meters (48.83), and as a member of the 4 × 400-meter relay team (3:18.29). The first American woman to win three Olympic gold medals in track since Wilma Rudolph in 1960, Valerie Brisco-Hooks carved out her own special place in Los Angeles, teaching all around her a few things about sacrifice and dedication, warmth and radiance. "I guess this proves you can come back from anything, even a baby," she said, and she laughed as tears came to her eyes again.

Brisco-Hooks won three gold medals in Los Angeles, impressing everybody with her warmth and radiance.

PAGES 252–253.
Winners of the 4 × 400 relay: Valerie Brisco-Hooks, Lilie Leatherwood, Sheri Howard and Chandra Cheeseborough.

Acknowledgments

In 1978 my first book, *Sports,* was published. For me, it was a dream come true. I moved on to *Time* magazine that year and assumed that my days on the sidelines and my ringside seat were gone forever. I'd taken sports pictures for 17 years, and now was the time to move on to presidents, mayors, popes, rock stars, space shuttles, and even subjects as far out as prisons. I've been very lucky since moving to *Time* because I have managed to explore so many of the new worlds I'd hoped to see up close. But a strange thing has happened these last seven years. I discovered that I still loved sports and sports photography. As a result, I never got too far away from shooting sports. There was Steve Cauthen, Bear Bryant, Eric Heiden, the World Cup in Argentina, and the Lake Placid Olympics. Sugar Ray Leonard became almost as wonderful a subject as Ali had been. Not quite — I still think of Ali as my all-time greatest subject. 1984 offered me what I consider the very best assignment I've had in my twenty-six years of taking pictures. I traveled to every place I'd ever dreamed of visiting, and as you can see from the photo essay that opens this book, I took some of the best pictures of my career. The Los Angeles Olympics provided many new sports stars (Mary Lou Retton, Carl Lewis, Daley Thompson, to name three) as well as terrific pictures. And so I'm getting a chance to do a sequel ("Dream Two" you can call it). This book has everything that has meant so much to me these last twenty-six years. Some of my old favorites, many of my all-time best pictures (which for some reason or another have never been published before), and the new ones which I hope are among my best work. I've just gotten my first look at the finished layouts for this book. J.C. Suarès — who designed the book — is very simply the best there is. He has made my pictures look better than I ever dreamed they could. I'm so proud of my "New Dream." I only wish my Dad were here to enjoy it with me. He was my toughest critic and my biggest fan. Thank you J.C. and thank you Pete Bonventre. It is not often that you get to collaborate with your best friend. Pete was asked to write a brief accompanying text. He did a lot more than that, and I think that he has made this book one of the best-written sports books ever. Another advantage of collaborating with Pete is that Dr. Martin

Bonventre, Pete's dad (and also his biggest booster), has promised to buy enough copies to ensure the success of this book even before publication.

I'm honored to have Roone Arledge do the foreword. I'm one of his biggest fans, and with two Olympics, a presidential election, and a Super Bowl all in one year, he's certainly been very busy. Thank you Roone for somehow finding the time and for helping to make this book so special.

Of course I haven't done this all by myself. I've had an awful lot of help. Ray Cave, my editor at *Time*: what can I say about him other than that he is the very best friend any photographer ever dreamed of having. I would never be where I am today were it not for Ray's never-ending support. He's always made me look better than I had any right to. Arnold Drapkin and Michele Stephenson, I promise you that nobody has ever had better bosses. Arnold and Michele have given me every possible opportunity to succeed. Demi Kosters (someone who would never toot her own horn) has given me so much support and patience that there is no way I could ever repay her. And most important, there's Tony Suarez—my friend and for the last seven years my assistant. It surely seems like modesty on my part (but I know better) when I say that many of my best pictures (Tony assisted me on my entire Olympic essay) are the direct result of Tony's hard work and total dedication. Tony's reward came in January when he was promoted to Staff Photographer. I hope he's lucky enough to find an assistant that's as good to him as he's been to me. Special thanks must also go to Jay Moses of ABC, and to Jim Fitzgerald at Dolphin/Doubleday who's been behind this book from the very beginning. Frank Micelotta's assistance in organizing and editing the pictures for this book was invaluable. Since so many of these pictures were taken before I came to *Time* I want also to be sure to thank Johnny Iacono, Manny Millan, Al Szabo, and the late Anthony Donna for the help they gave me.

Last but not least, Corey, Jodie, Renae, and Mom, thanks.

Neil Leifer

Fidel Castro lighting my cigar? Is that really Castro? Is that really me? *It's been 25 years since I began as a photographer and yet I still have to pinch myself to believe many of the wonderful things that my good fortune and my camera have opened up to me. My ticket to the world and to so many of my dreams has always been my camera. My father always called photography "a rich man's hobby." He wanted me to be a doctor or a lawyer. He was a very wise man, but he was wrong about my photography. As you can surely see from the pictures in this book, "my ticket," a.k.a. my camera, has been very, very good to me. I consider myself extremely lucky, and I hope that I've been able to bring others some of the enjoyment that my camera has brought me.*

—Neil Leifer
May 1985